T0129959

OTHER BOOKS AUTHORED BY DR OLERIBE INCLUDE

- Repositioning for Marital Success
- Celebrating Marital Success
- Making Maximum Impact in Life – The Keys
- Transforming Ideas, Seed for Entrepreneurship and Greatness
- Vital Leadership Thoughts and Nuggets
- The Concept of Child Abuse
- Fundamentals of Child Rights
- ADJS at 40: Celebrating Excellence, Consolidating the Vision (Editor)

SCALING
NEW HEIGHTS

Based on Life Principles from the Bible

OBINNA OSITADIMMA OLERIBE

authorHOUSE®

AuthorHouse™
1663 Liberty Drive
Bloomington, IN 47403
www.authorhouse.com
Phone: 1 (800) 839-8640

Published by AuthorHouse 11/27/2019

ISBN: 978-1-7283-3603-9 (sc)
ISBN: 978-1-7283-3601-5 (hc)
ISBN: 978-1-7283-3602-2 (e)

Library of Congress Control Number: 2019918707

Print information available on the last page.

Scripture quotations marked KJV are from the Holy Bible, King James Version (Authorized Version). First published in 1611. Quoted from the KJV Classic Reference Bible, Copyright © 1983 by The Zondervan Corporation.

This book is printed on acid-free paper.

DEDICATED

This book is dedicated to my Sons – Alpha
Chimgozirim and Winner Chimkaneme
And to
All my sons and daughters in ministry

God has already empowered and equipped you
for higher heights than whatever we attained

Go for it.

CONTENTS

PREFACE

This is a product of over five years of personal meditation, office presentations and blogs. I have read the bible several times and each time, the Word is new with new insights and revelations.

Initially, I was sharing this in my office devotion every Monday morning (8.00 – 9.00 am). Later, by the help of a staff – Shola Oke – we started publishing these in my blog as Monday Manner.

I had a leading to compile these into a book for someone – like you – to read, meditate, reflect and apply. I believe that the contents of this book will not only bless you, but also energize you for new heights.

What you will discover from this book is not the conventional things you will hear from the altar. NO. This is new, this is unique and this is easily applicable to our daily lives.

I am sure you will identify with some of the topics and chapters more. So, feel free to go to the chapter that interests you most. But try and walk your way all through the various sections and chapters. Related topics were deliberately grouped into Parts 1 to 5. There is no criteria for this grouping. So, feel free to see them from your own perspective.

Join me to thank **Mr Chisom O Anukam** for proof reading the manuscript, and making valuable contributions to this work. I look forward to hearing from you after reading and applying these nuggets.

God will give you the needed grace, not only to read but to apply each and every segment of the book towards the new heights you deserve.

God bless you.

INTRODUCTION

The best time to think about, plan, and actually work towards new heights is when things seem not to be working. Life is a RACE. Everybody is either running from something or running towards something. Some are running from poverty while others are running to prosperity; some are running from sickness and diseases, while others are running towards wholesomeness and divine health; some are running from nightmares, while others are running towards their dreams; some are running from bad partnerships, while others are running towards new partnerships; some are running from disappointments, while others are running into their appointments; some are running from regrets, while others are running into opportunities. Everyone is on the run – to or from something.

I do not know which one describes you – or maybe I completely missed your case, but you are also on a race. But a race not well defined can lead into avoidable errors. A race without a destination can be disastrous and very destructive. A race without an end in sight can be frustrating and stress-full. Thus, we must define the destination of our own race.

The truth is that you cannot feature in the future you cannot picture. In this book, I will be able to, by the help of the Holy

Spirit, guide you into a desirable destination as scaling new heights should be and *is* everybody's assignment and reality.

Where are you currently in life? Where do you want to be in the future? Have you properly defined, designed, and developed the strategies towards achieving your dreams? This book will serve as a guide and motivation towards your next level – a new height in life, career, ministry, finances, and even relationship.

I have assembled a number of my articles over the past five years in this book. They are Holy Ghost inspired. I will make some minor changes to ensure they remain relevant. Join me on this walk into New Heights. Before we get into the main book, let me introduce you to KEY.

Recently, I got acquainted with a new definition of the word, KEY, which strongly resonated with me. In this book, I will be putting into your hands the key to scaling new heights if Key is taken as Knowingly Educating Yourself. However, if you are already educated in how to scale new Heights, then for you KEY will mean, Knowingly Enlightening Yourself. Are you enlightened already and enough? Then Knowingly Energize or Empower Yourself! Are you already energized and empowered, then KEY for you will be Knowingly Entertaining Yourself. Allow me to therefore either educate, enlighten, energize, empower or entertain you with the following articles spread across the chapters of this book. Accept this KEY from me as my contribution towards your next height in life. Let us *scale new heights* together.

Let the journey into scaling new heights begin.

WE ALL HAVE 24/7

Time is the greatest resource in life.

While some use theirs to make wealth, others use theirs to get poorer

While some use theirs to build destinies, others use theirs to destroy their destinies

We all have 24/7

Time cannot be stopped

Time cannot be stockpiled

Time cannot be stretched

Time can only be used

But we all have 24/7

You waste your time, you waste life

You while it away...it grows wings and flies

You spend your time, you lose it

You invest your time, it yields you 30, 60 or 100 fold returns in life

People's attitude to time determines their attitude to life

People are low because they are slow

People lack, because they slack

People beg, because they build on wasted times

We all have 24/7

What are you doing with your 24/7?

Sleeping – majority sleep for more than one third of their lives

Watching – while others make money

Watching – while others make news 24/7

Time is going…are you getting better?

24/7 is all you have.

Invest it.

PART 1

RUN TO OBTAIN

CHAPTER 1

LIFE AS A RACE

Genesis 32: 24-29

²⁴ And Jacob was left alone; and there wrestled a man with him until the breaking of the day. ²⁵ And when he saw that he prevailed not against him, he touched the hollow of his thigh; and the hollow of Jacob's thigh was out of joint, as he wrestled with him. ²⁶ And he said, Let me go, for the day breaketh. And he said, I will not let thee go, except thou bless me. ²⁷ And he said unto him, What is thy name? And he said, Jacob. ²⁸ And he said, Thy name shall be called no more Jacob, but Israel: for as a prince hast thou power with God and with men, and hast prevailed. ²⁹ And Jacob asked him, and said, Tell me, I pray thee, thy name. And he said, Wherefore is it that thou dost ask after my name? And he blessed him there.

Life is a race. Everyone is in this race. However, although everyone is running in this race, success in life's race is individually determined. We may run a relay race with each playing his/her part; however, most life's races are individual race. Like Jacob, in this race of life, there comes a time when you are on your own – father and mother have left you, brothers and sisters have abandoned you. Uncles and aunts who made promises to you have failed you. You are just alone. Friends in school, in church and in recreational centres are nowhere to be found. At such a time as this, unless you run, you will perish. Unless you race with all you have in you, you may be erased out of life and destiny.

Therefore, friends, run the race of life! To succeed in this race, there are seven things you must take note of;

1. **Keep dreaming**: Everyone in a race must have a vision of his/her destination – the finish line of the race. What is your vision, mission and dream? At some point in time, you had big dreams. You must have achieved some of these dreams. Maybe some did not come to pass, I encourage you to dream again. In dreaming again, you must fight for your dreams in other for it to come to pass. Dreams are always contested by Satan. Do not just sit down and cross your legs and hope your dreams will come to pass. Everything around you may not support your goal, everything around you may even contradict your plans, but you must move against the tide. Dream again, fight for your dreams, and work to see your dreams come to pass.

2. **Believe in your dreams**: You cannot fight for a dream you do not believe in. A wise man said "If you do not fight for something, you will fall for anything". Have a reason for living. The Bible calls it purpose.

Go out and find your purpose, believe in it, and you will achieve it when you act on it.

3. **Act on your dreams**: Stand up and act, have strategies and plans. Map out strategies on how to execute your plans to achieve your dreams. No matter how big/small your dream is, believe in it, have a strategy, and act to achieve it. Plan and make sure you follow through with your plans.

4. **Keep learning, unlearning and re-learning**: In executing your plans, you must be able to learn and unlearn. Sit back and review your actions, learn what should be learnt and discard practices that are bad. If you do something the same way over and over again, do not expect to get a different result; only fools do that. Learn new things regularly.

5. **Keep reasoning**: Have a thinking time. It could be very early in the morning when you wake up or late at night before going to bed. Whatever the time may be, ensure you map out a private time to reason. You should not just think, think logically. Some people just worry and call it thinking - you must think strategically. Reason out your dreams. Think out steps that work. Chunk up, chunk down thoughts to get new ideas.

6. **Work out your plan**: Yes, it is good to have a dream, plan for it and reason out strategies. However, to get this dream actualized, you must work it out. Work out your plan and strategies. Take your plans from articles of faith on paper to expressions of reality.

7. **Keep praying**: No matter how good your plan is, no matter how terrific the strategies you have mapped out are, no matter the connections you have, you

need God on your side because without him you can do nothing. It is God's blessings that make riches and add no sorrows. It is only with God that one can have sweat free breakthroughs. Without God in your plans, you will miss it as it is God that will lay His hands of blessings upon you to make you excel.

To be successful in this race; keep dreaming and let your dreams drive you every day, week and month. Take steps in line with your dream, learn new ways of doing things (get skills), reason your way out of all difficulties and challenges; and work until your dreams are realized. Work and partner with God to see your dreams realized.

CHAPTER 2

ALLOW YOURSELF TO BE GUIDED

Revelation 22:1

And he shewed me a pure river of water of life, clear as crystal, proceeding out of the throne of God and of the Lamb

In this race of life, we need guidance. This is brand new journey. You do not know the way to your destination. You do not have the capacity or skills to get there by yourself. As there are things you may never see – no matter how hard you try, swallow your pride and understand that you need to be guided! There was a young girl called Hagar who bore a child for Abraham. She was on a journey with her young son in the wilderness and ran out of water. When she couldn't bear to watch her child die of thirst, she abandoned him under a shrub and sat afar off watching and waiting for the baby to die. The Lord heard the cry of the lad and spoke to her. He just guided her with his words, and she saw a pool of water. She gave water to her thirsty baby and and she also drank (Genesis 21: 8-21). They were both refreshed and revived!

There are times when good things are all around you, but you cannot see them until someone shows them to you. Allow yourself to be guided. You may think you know enough. But friends, there are always new things to learn and see. I do not care how well you are currently doing, you can always do better. Some years ago, I was in Ibadan to do an update course during my residency training. I stayed in a friend's house. There was a girl staying in the adjoining room. She was the one who gave us food and took care of our needs. My host had a fiancée he wanted to marry. When he complained to me about his predicaments and challenges in his current relationship, I just asked him to look inwards, as what he was looking for may literally be waiting for him next door. His eyes were opened and he saw the beautiful wife God kept for him at his doorstep. Today, they are married with four wonderful children.

There are individuals who God will send your way as destiny helpers. Do not close your eyes to them. Some of us are so fixed to our ideas that we have refused to open our eyes to learn from others. If you are in an organization with 25-35 staff, you can learn something new from everybody, every week. You can learn how to do something or how not to do things. You can learn best practices. In life, you struggle when you want to discover everything yourself. Let somebody ahead of you show you the way.

Allow yourself to learn, let somebody show you what you do not know. Feel free to go to someone and ask how they do things and achieve better results. Allow yourself to be guided. Towards the end of every day, week, month or year, ask yourself, "What did I learn today or this week/month/year?" It takes learning to earn. There is no easy way to earn. You must learn to earn otherwise 2 to 3 years from now, you would still be wondering, complaining and murmuring, asking "why am I not doing this?" Learn therefore, to do better. Allow someone to show you things you do not (and may never) know. Open yourself to learn how to do things the easier way. When you do this, the sky will become your starting point.

Why should someone show You?

1. **Because they have gone ahead of you**: You do not need to reinvent the wheel. You do not have to struggle or begin to think of how to do things that have already been done. Ask those who have already done it to show you the way.

2. **It reduces your learning curve**: Learning from others reduces the amount of years you spend learning some things. When I began my doctorate degree at Walden University, I called a female student to take me through the process. In less than 60 minutes, she gave me the tools that accelerated my program and made me complete the course in just 24 months!

3. **It guarantees exploits:** When you climb on the shoulders of those who have gone ahead, you would see better. Isaac Newton said, "If I have seen

farther than others, it is because I was standing on the shoulder of giants." Learning from others guarantees exploits.

4. **It reduces frustrations and improves success rates**: Life is full of frustrations and roller coaster of highs and lows – but this can be minimized by learning from others. Learn as much as you can from those around you, to abate your frustrations.

When we allow those ahead of us to guide us, we enjoy God's blessings.

CHAPTER 3

THE CURRENCY FOR SUCCESS

Let me begin by debunking a few myths about success.

Myth 1: Only a few can succeed: Success is available to all, but achieved by a few. Anybody can succeed – if they are willing to pay the price. But as a few are willing to pay this price – few end up succeeding.

Myth 2: People succeed based on the resources available to them: People are not successful due to how much money they have in their accounts – irrespective of the currency or denomination. With the current whistle blowing going on in Nigeria, anybody who has access to information can make millions over night! This is not a measure of true success. Discovering a huge sum of money stolen by someone (perhaps a former associate) across the nation, blowing the whistle, and getting rewarded for it does not equate to success.

Myth 3: You must be connected to be successful: Your connection with your father, mother, or uncle is not enough to guarantee your success. Being a child of God is a plus, but that again does not guarantee success in life.

Myth 4: You must be educated to be successful: Success is not a function of qualifications. A few weeks ago, we went for an outreach and my colleague met a man with a PhD of over 16 years who was unemployed, and thus unable to manage his life challenges. We met him jobless, smoking and drinking.

Myth 5: Success runs in the blood: Your lineage is not a guarantee for your success. That your father or mother did well does not mean you would do well and vice versa. Many children of the highly successful have ended up as colossal failures.

What then is the currency for success? This currency for success succeeds in every nation of the world. Everywhere people are found, it is a valid means of transaction.

2 Kings 10:16:

And he said, Come with me, and see my zeal for the Lord. So they made him ride in his chariot.

The currency for success is zeal. Zeal is a vital force that guarantees success. You can see, touch and feel zeal in a person.

According to the Merriam-Webster dictionary, *zeal is the great energy or enthusiasm in pursuit of a cause or an objective.* Show me a zealous man and I will show you a man that is ready to succeed in life. Zeal gives colour to

10

your life and beauty to your destiny. Zeal is what makes life meaningful. Where there is no zeal, there is no life. Even if you are deaf and dumb, if you have zeal, you will make it in life. If you know nothing at all, have nothing to your name, but you are zealous, you will do well in life. Give me a man that has zeal and nothing else, I will make him a star in a few years; but give me someone that has a first class and no zeal, there is no way he will succeed in the real world.

Many of us are down because we are not zealous about anything. For us it is *"que sera sera - whatever shall be shall be".* *"If I go to work what shall be shall be, if I come back home what shall be shall be. If I write exams and pass or fail what shall be shall be."* Hear me again, as long as your life lacks zeal, your destiny will lack colour! It is your zeal in life that gives colour to your destiny!

In every area of life; career, marriage, or ministry, it is your zeal that makes all the difference. You do not just go around saying you have zeal, your zeal should be seen from your actions. This past weekend someone walked into my office and saw me working. He said, "why are you here working, you should be home resting". I told him employees work Mondays to Fridays but employers of labour work 24/7. It is not because we are so strong, but it is our zeal that keeps us going and working while others are resting.

Christ said, "the zeal of your house has consumed me" (Psalm 69:9, John 2:17). No wonder he came to the world and succeeded in his life mission and today, over 2000 years after his death, the whole world is still celebrating him. What consumes you? What keeps you awake at night? What is that thing that keeps your heart racing? What is that thing that except it is done, you do not have peace? What is that thing that moves you? What is that thing you are so good at and you would be missed for if you are absent?

Any day you appear at work without the right "zeal-set" just go back home because you can be an impediment to the success of that day. There are two kinds of men in the world today; those who are zealous and those who are not. This also means that there are those who will succeed - having the right zeal-set - and those who will surely fail - lacking this zeal-set. These two kinds of people are manifested in Isaiah 29:8, 11, 12

8 It shall even be as when an hungry man dreameth, and, behold, he eateth; but he awaketh, and his soul is empty: or as when a thirsty man dreameth, and, behold, he drinketh; but he awaketh, and, behold, he is faint, and his soul hath appetite:....

There are the **dreamers** and the **darers**. Those who dream to do all manner of great things but never do anything; and those who dare any and everything. Zeal makes you a darer and the absence of zeal makes you a mere dreamer.

In verses 11 and 12, the prophet said; *11 And the vision of all is become unto you as the words of a book that is sealed, which men deliver to one that is learned, saying, Read this, I pray thee: and he saith, I cannot; for it is sealed: 12 And the book is delivered to him that is not learned, saying, Read this, I pray thee: and he saith, I am not learned.*

To one that is learned, it is sealed; to the other who is not learned, he is not learned. Friends, lack of zeal manifests in multiple excuses. To every human being there is a reason not to do what you ought to do. The excuses of life are the manifestations of *zeallessness*. If you must succeed, you need zeal and must be zealous. It is what you are zealous for that you would be known for. If you live your life taking life as it is, you would live a very nominal life without adding any value to yourself or to your world.

Be zealous, over a billion people are worshipping God through Jesus Christ today because many years ago the zeal of God's house consumed Him. It took zeal for Him to die. Paul never met Christ, but today he is one of the most outstanding Apostles because he had zeal which made him stand out.

Hear Paul in 1 Corinthians 15:10: *¹⁰ But by the grace of God I am what I am: and his grace which was bestowed upon me was not in vain; but I laboured more abundantly than they all: yet not I, but the grace of God which was with me.*

Grace only meets you on your way to success when your zeal is intact. No matter how qualified, rich or beautiful you think you are, if you lack zeal, your life will lack meaning. What attracts people to you is the zeal you manifest. Your zeal manifests as your passion and it is what makes people listen to what you have to say. When people say, "I want to be like you", I ask them **"are you willing to do**

what I have done in life?" Being like me is not a prayer point, it is hard work.

From now henceforth, find something you would be zealous for and go to work.

CHAPTER 4

WHO OR WHAT DEFINES YOU?

Who or what defines you? Are you defined by your name, for instance, Obinna, Smith, etc.; your physical appearance (your looks, weight, height, complexion); your socio-economic status (the economy, amount of money in your pocket/bank account); your marital status (married, single, divorcee, widow etc.); your dress sense; your tribe or friends; your qualifications (SSCE, HND, BSC, MSC, PGD, PHD); your religion (African religion, Christianity, Islam etc.); personal activities (efforts, errors, successes, failures etc.); or by the circumstance of or challenges in life?

Who/what defines you? This is a question we all need to answer; otherwise, we will end up having a lot of issues in life. *Who/what defines you?*

Job 12:1,3 says: **And Job answered and said, ² No doubt but ye are the people, and wisdom shall die with you. ³ But I have understanding as well as you; I am not inferior to you: yea, who knoweth not such things as these?**

In Job 13:2 he repeated the same by saying; ² *what ye know, the same do I know also: I am not inferior unto you.*

Job was a man with a lot of challenges; his friends came around him to define him based on his current trials and tribulations. But he will not let them. He made them to understand that, despite his circumstance, he still knew who he was - he was not *inferior* to them.

Many of us lose our peace, self-esteem and feel worthless because of what people say to us or around us. Friends, who/what defines you? Job lost all he had, his children (7 sons and 3 daughters), his wealth and health, yet he told his friends who came to define him that though he was down with pain and sores all over his body "he was not inferior to them". That is a man who did not allow life circumstances to define him. Why? because he knew that the physical structure seen is just a container that houses the real you. *Who defines you?*

Who or what do you allow to define you? Not married, so you lose your peace? Yet to have a child, so you lose your peace? Not having a job, or not having a car, so you lose your peace? You hide where you live from people because you are afraid of what people would say. Who defines you? God made you the way you are for a particular purpose and you must understand that life is more than the clothes you wear or the way you look. People will always have their opinions about you, and friends, you can't stop them. So, don't die because of it. Just understand who you are.

Allow me to show you the true definition of who you are. You are not defined by your circumstances, qualifications, looks, the amount of money you have in your bank account, or by your social status. You are defined by God himself.

In Matthew 11:11, Jesus said this: ***Verily I say unto you, among them that are born of women there hath not risen anyone greater than John the Baptist: notwithstanding he that is least in the kingdom of heaven is greater than he.***

If you are born-again and truly a child of God, you are greater than Isaiah, Ezekiel, Daniel, Jeremiah, Moses, and all the prophets of old. Some people pray for the wisdom of Daniel. That is an insult to you because the wisdom of Daniel should be your baseline. Friends, you have more access to God than Elijah because you are greater than them all.

He went further to explain what he meant in John 14:12 by saying – in case you do not understand what it means to be greater than John the Baptist; *¹² **Verily, verily, I say unto you, He that believeth on me, the works that I do shall he do also; and greater works than these shall he do; because I go unto my Father.***

Therefore, even when you are on the floor, understand that you are not meant for the floor. There is something greater in you, there is something in and about you that is about to burst forth. Jesus said, *"the works I do shall you do and greater works shall you do because I go to my Father"*, that's who you are. In case you don't understand what that means, Peter puts it in a very interesting way.

1Peter 2:9 say: [9] *But ye are a chosen generation, a royal priesthood, an holy nation, a peculiar people; that ye should shew forth the praises of him who hath called you out of darkness into his marvellous light;*

You are a royal priesthood, a holy nation, a peculiar person, and a chosen generation. You are not a common or ordinary being. In all these things your height, size, marital status, qualifications were not mentioned because what you carry inside of you is more than what the world can give you. Don't allow anybody born of a woman or any devil from hell to make you feel less than who you are. You have the authority of God to make a difference on earth.

Therefore, don't live like a second-class citizen or like a photocopy of who you should be. Be yourself, stand out among your pairs, anywhere you find yourself, occupy your position. Don't allow anybody make you feel inferior when you should be superior. Don't get intimidated or get self-marginalized but understand who you are.

Don't allow your parents, background, house, qualifications, husband/wife, team lead/members or anybody anywhere make you feel inferior.

You need to understand who you are and not be limited by who people think you are if you want to scale new heights! If you do, you will not walk with your head bowed down. God will give you the grace to live a fulfilled life knowing who you are, in Jesus Name.

CHAPTER 5

THE FOUR FACES OF MAN

The book of Ezekiel, chapter 10 recorded one of the many visions revealed to the Prophet, Ezekiel. Many of us do not enjoy the book of Ezekiel because of its abstractness. But friends, allow me, by the Holy Spirit to discuss with you the four faces of man from one of his visions.

Ezekiel 10:14: *And every one had four faces: the first face was the face of a cherub, and the second face was the face of a man, and the third the face of a lion, and the fourth the face of an eagle*

Everyone has four faces. In life, to succeed, be a total man, and scale new heights, we must show these four faces. A complete understanding, expression and balance of these faces help you become a successful man.

The first face is the face of the cherub. This depicts the spiritual aspect of man. Bishop Oyedepo defines man as a **spirit** that has a **soul** and live in a **body**. Every man whether Christian, Muslim, or atheist is a spirit being and has a higher authority he/she respects. This higher authority some believe to be God, Allah, Amadioha, an inner chi, whatsoever. Most people have higher authorities they respect and report to. The first face lays a foundation for the spiritual. Friends, the advancement and exploits you do in life determines your success spiritually.

The second face is the face of man. This depicts the natural face; our life as humans; our relationships with people, our emotions, well-being, health, career etc. Everything that makes us human is included in this face. The better we are able to handle this face, the better our relationships with people will be, and the better our lives in general on earth will be.

The third face of man is the face of a lion. This is our inner warrior. The lion represents our ability to struggle in life, fight and hustle for the things we want. The lion in us is our will power to do things to move ourselves forward. If we do not find that inner lion in us and stir it up, friends we will certainly live a life of mediocrity, shying away from challenges and swimming in the shallow waters of life.

The fourth and final face is the face of the eagle. The face of the eagle depicts our successful self. It depicts career success, marital success, financial success, etc. After we have been able to lay a proper foundation with the cherub face, balanced the human face and discover the lion within us, the face of the eagle begins to manifest. The eagle connotes our all-round success in life.

Friends the ability to effectively manifest these four faces in life will bring about verse 22 of that scripture in our lives.

Ezekiel 14:22*And the likeness of their faces was the same faces which I saw by the river of Chebar, their appearances and themselves: they went every one straight forward.*

We experience advancement and fulfil destiny when we are on top of the four faces – with God as our spiritual head. We can look back on our lives in our old age and smile to ourselves satisfactorily knowing we have truly maximized our destiny and ready to die empty. God shall give us the grace to identify our four faces in life and fully express them in Jesus name.

CHAPTER 6

THREE TYPES OF MEN

In life, there can never be two fully identical people in the world, so even as our looks are different so also are our choices. You may come from the same family, where one may be doing so well and others are not doing well at all. It is not a result of the gene, but the choices they made. It is important we know that, there are three kinds of people in the world.

I want to begin by talking to you about one of them as documented in the book of Joshua 17:14-16 saying,

14 And the children of Joseph spake unto Joshua, saying, Why hast thou given me but one lot and one portion to inherit, seeing I am a great people, forasmuch as the Lord hath blessed me hitherto? 15 And Joshua answered them, if thou be a great people, then get thee up to the wood country, and cut down for thyself there in the land of the Perizzites and of the giants, if mount Ephraim be too narrow for thee. 16 And the children of Joseph said, the hill is not enough for us: and all the Canaanites that dwell in the land

of the valley have chariots of iron, both they who are of Bethshean and her towns, and they who are of the valley of Jezreel.

Complainers. They are always complaining about any and everything. Do you know who I am? Do you know my qualification(s)? Do you know where I come from? Do you know I have twenty-five or forty-five years' experience, why this irrelevant position? They are Ephraimites. They feel too big and always complain – the office, their salary, cleaners, caterers, family members, bathroom, bedsheet, work tools, vehicle, just everything. They are Ephraimites. They are full of themselves and are never satisfied with what they have. More importantly, they are never willing to lift up their fingers to change their situation. They just believe that anybody and everybody should do things for them!

Joshua said unto them go up to the mountain and take over the city. Joshua saw wood but they saw chariots - iron chariots. This kind of people always find excuses why they cannot do what they ought to do to change their present situations. They give reasons to justify their laziness and their stupidity. They are the Ephraimites. They always have a good reason for every failure in life. My prayer is that none of us shall end up as Ephraimites. Things may be difficult, I agree. Things maybe hard, I agree. But people are making progress in the so-called difficult period. Don't be an Ephraimite, otherwise you will live and die from mourning and complaining, and nothing will ever change.

The second type of people is found in;

Joshua 19:9

9 Out of the portion of the children of Judah was the inheritance of the children of Simeon: for the part of the children of Judah was too much for them: therefore the children of Simeon had their inheritance within the inheritance of them.

Parasites, at best commensals. *...therefore, the children of Simeon had their inheritance within the inheritance of* other people. Simeonites are always parasites, looking for where to attach, rather than creating or opening opportunities for themselves. They are always looking for those people that already have what they want, and they just attach themselves. They attach themselves with others for houses, breakfast, lunch and everything, they are the Simeonites. Don't be a parasite. Giving is never wrong; giving and sharing is beautiful. However, sharing should not be overlooked. It should not be a one-way affair but should be reciprocated.

Don't be a Simeonite or a parasite, so that when you come around people, they will not be afraid. Also, never allow the Simeonites around you, because they will always be looking for how to gain from you but will not give, or add value to you. Yes, Judah had a large place which is beyond what he needed; but friends, there is no law that says Simeon should not get their own equally large land. But, forever, they chose to be servants to Judah and to be attaché in the large place of Judah.

Remember that the first kinds of people are the Ephraimites who are always complaining and mourning about everything but will never lift their hands to secure that change they desire. The second kind of people are the Simeonites that are constantly looking for who they will benefit from without any plans of giving back, looking for where they will not have to labour or fight for anything, where things are always ready. This is hardly the right way to live. That is why I am introducing you to the third group of people.

Initiators and step-takers!

Joshua 19:47 *And the coast of the children of Dan went out too little for them: therefore the children of Dan went up to fight against Leshem, and took it, and smote it with the edge of the sword, and possessed it, and dwelt therein, and called Leshem, Dan, after the name of Dan their father.*

Be a Danite! Nobody told them to do anything, they took initiatives. They were not happy with their present situation – they took steps and made a difference! Stop complaining. Stop looking for cheap or easy way out. Stop living off people. Be a Danite. Take steps, be proactive, be the change you want to see. And scale new heights.

While Ephramites were complaining, Danites were conquering territories to immortalize their father's name. Choose to be a Danite – go for what you want, fight for what you desire, dispossess all false occupiers to possess your inheritances. The idea of sitting around waiting for things to come your way is childishness and obsolete; you have a battle to fight. It takes battles fought and won to scale new heights.

Danites got and dwelt in a large place, why? Because they were willing to fight their battles, and were very willing to go the extra mile. They were very willing to do what the Ephraimites and the Simeonite were not willing to do. If you think your location is too small then enlarge it, expand it, increase it. **This is the Danite's Principle.**

Begin to think beyond where you are right now. There are greater things for each of us. You can be a staff and be a farmer. I recently heard about an 'illiterate' Nigerian who desired to be a rice farmer. To actualize his dreams, he began to acquire lands in his community – and today (over a period of 30 years), he has more than 28,000 hectares of land to farm rice. Vision is not a one day affair, it's a lifelong commitment. Don't fold your hands and wait for the day things will turn around, it doesn't happen that way. Anywhere you are right now, you can add something else to yourself. You can spend your time more wisely, you can do something better. Remember, greatness is not a 100 meters dash, it is a lifelong marathon. Begin today – if you are yet to start - and choose to scale new heights.

CHAPTER 7

UNDERSTANDING THE YOU IN YOU

Several times we allow ourselves to be guided and controlled by the things we hear or see around us. These make us to look down on ourselves and who we are. To scale new heights, you must know the you in you.

Psalm 82:5

⁵ They know not, neither will they understand; they walk on in darkness: all the foundations of the earth are out of course.

Every time you are ignorant of the you that you are, then your foundation becomes unstable. Every time you are ignorant of who you are, you become a subject of people's mockery and their pity. They know not - no wonder the bible says; my people are destroyed for the lack of knowledge (Hosea 4:6). When you lack understanding of who you are, then every wind blows you to every corner.

⁶ I have said, Ye are gods; and all of you are children of the most High.

God has said ye are gods. Jesus said "Is it not written in your scriptures that ye are gods?" (John 10:34). Who is a god and what are his characteristics?

A god has authority, dominion, power, ability to rule, is creative, full of love, eternal, faithful and merciful. Let me in the next few paragraphs explain a few of these.

As a god;

> ➤ **You have dominion:** God has given us power to trample upon serpents and scorpions, and over all the power of the enemy, and nothing shall by any means harm us (Luke 10:19). We have dominion over every negative habit, sickness, witches and wizards. We have dominion over everything and anything that we do not like.
>
> However, many have limited themselves because of fear. Because of fear, many may not give their money or gifts to those in need, do not shake hands, do not travel to their home-lands, or visit their relations. We forget that by the law of diffusion, power flows from a higher level to a lower level and not the other way around. So, if you're harmed by handshakes, you are not strong. Remember that you have dominion over Satan and all his agents!
>
> ➤ **You have the capacity to be creative**: You were made by God a co-creator in the affairs of men.

Everything you see today was created by men and women like you and I. People have created houses, cars, dresses, shoes, phones, airplanes, ships, computers, internet, watches, etc. All these are created by people like you and I. God will never come down and create anything again. That's why he has us as co-creators in the affairs of life. Turning a whole bush into an estate, looking at what isn't working and making it to work, seeing someone dying and giving them life are some of the things God expects you and I to do. When people see you, they should have hope. When people call your number, they are calling you because they expect you will make a difference in their lives; You are God's co-creators. Just as you call upon God everyday in prayers believing he will answer, when people call you, they should have hope that things will change around them.

➢ **You are a preservative:** God sustains everything by his word. There has not been any decadence in the world since He made it. The Bible says that we are the salt of the earth, the light of the world (Matthew 5:13-16). What does salt do? Salt adds taste and preserves. We can't afford to go down from where we are now, we have to go up because we are gods. We have the capacity to create something new in every phase of our lives. We are a people who have dominion over all that is not working and have the ability to make it work. YE ARE GODS.

➢ **We have divine nature**: If you die now, you're still alive as only your body dies. We should build everlasting things. Build systems that run into hundreds of years and can stand the test of time.

We should work to leave legacies for our children's children.

Life is more than what we see right now. The Bible says "ye are gods". Let the gods in us manifest. God is self-motivate as no one motivates God. He is who He is, he changeth not. It is not what you do to God that makes him who He is. It is an inherent nature of God to *be* God. Anywhere you are found, beginning from today, let the God in you emerge. Let people see you as one that has dominion over everything, one that has the capacity to create new things, one that has the capacity to preserve things, and one that has the divine nature to make things eternal. Let people see you, not just as what you look like right now, but let the true you emerge. Let solutions emerge and let possibilities arrive with you, then the god in you will be manifested.

Ye are gods. If you don't know and understand that, then verse 7 becomes a reality;

7 But ye shall die like men, and fall like one of the princes.

I pray that this will never be our portion. We shall shoot above our peers as this god status is not a function of qualifications, family background, or how much you have. It is a function of your belief in God's word. If God the father is truly your father, then you are a god. Anywhere you find yourself at any time, ask **yourself "if God was to be here, what will happen?"** and then go ahead and make it happen. Take-over, take dominion and return with excellent results that will surprise you. I pray that the God in us will henceforth be made fully manifest.

CHAPTER 8

ABOVE OR BELOW THE LINE

There is a line of life. This line demarcates those doing well from those who are not; the successful from the failure, the rich from the poor, and those who are living from those who are merely existing. On the scale of life, anyone below or equal to 5 (i.e. 0 – 5) is below this line; while all those above 5 (i.e. 6 – 10) are above the line. Among all those below the line, some may be as bad as zero, while others may be closer to the line at 5. However, all those below the line have similar characteristics and results. Those above the line could be anywhere between 6 and 10. Although very few people can make 10 which is the ultimate goal of the wise, brave and progressive.

Are you below or above the line? If you are below the line, you merely exist. Life for you is a burden. You have reasons/excuses why things are not working. You actually consciously and otherwise remove yourself from the A-list. You therefore live an average or mediocre life. However, the good news is that you can change your position – and work to move above the line. This is why you must scale new heights.

We live in a world where people claim every prophecy, prayer, and word on social media. Friends, success in life takes much more than mere claiming prayers and prophecies. It requires work, commitment and focus. Success requires deliberate desire to go above the line. Have you ever watched a high jumper in action? They deliberately step backwards, assess the height of the bar, decide how far backwards they must go, take deliberate initial steps, then run to scale the height. Heights are scaled by deliberate steps taken consciously by individuals who desire to make significant marks in life.

If you are above the line, congratulations. You have made a difference or are currently making a difference. The good news is that you can do more. If you are below the line, you must desire to change location, and if above, choose to make more impact.

What is this line? This line is the line of average, mediocrity and limitations. Those below this line **BEND**.

First, they **B**lame others (parents, uncles, peers, relations, or even the government) for their failures or inability to rise in life. To those who live below this line, everything that happens to them is someone else's fault. But any good thing that happens is their hard-work. People who live below the line blame even inanimate objectives for negative occurrences e.g. accidents, burnt food, etc. The danger of this is they never see any fault in what they do and are quick to refuse corrections, rebuke correctors, and remain in their comfort zone despite the realities in their lives.

Secondly, individuals below this line daily give **E**xcuses. They give excuses for all their failures, inability to achieve, and continuous loss of opportunities. They excuse their weaknesses, bad behaviours, unhealthy relationships, lateness to events, and even their mistakes and errors. They excuse everything.

Thirdly, they **N**ag. Individuals below the line nag about almost everything. They nag their spouses, children, friends, and even helpers of their destinies. Their nagging is on almost everything and this scares people away from them.

Finally, individuals below the line live in **D**enial. They have challenges but deny its existence. They have weaknesses, but refuse to accept them. They deny facts and run with the shadow, fantasies and fictions.

Living below the line destroys potentials, excellence and initiative. If all the components of **BEND** are seen in you, you are close to zero in the scale of life. However, if only one or two are prominent in you, then you are close to 5.

On the other hand, those above the line are successful, excited, enthusiastic and very proactive. They **ROAR**. They roar at their challenges, obstacles and situations. They do not deny the fact that things may be tough; they confront them to overcome them.

First, people above the line **R**ecognize their limitations and work hard to overcome them. Where it is not possible to overcome these obstacles, they leverage on other resources to attain their goals. They recognize opportunities and maximize them. They recognise their destiny helpers and go for them. They recognize their skills, talents and potentials and exploit them. They are doers and not mere talkers. They are proactive, creative and risk takers. These people see things before they happen and position themselves to enjoy rather than live through the change.

Secondly, they take **O**wnership of their successes or failures. One great strength of individuals above the line is that they do not blame, deny, neglect or excuse themselves from their challenges or current situations, rather, they take ownership of their challenges and work to solve them, overcome their weaknesses and work to eliminate bad habits. They learn from their failures and strive not to repeat them.

Thirdly, individuals above the line are **A**ccountable. They accept responsibility for their actions and inactions – and thus are very accountable to themselves and those around them. They are accountable to their employers, employees, spouse, children, government and relations. They account for their resources, time and talents. They also account for life opportunities and failures. They are accountable; they document and report.

Finally, above the line individuals are very **R**espectful and resourceful. They respect God and serve Him as the primary source of all good things including wisdom. They respect people who have gone ahead of them or done better than them and strive to learn from them. They respect their peers for horizontal learning, and spouses as key partners in progress. These individuals are always respectful of the laws, constitution/rules of the organization, institution and community. Above all, they are resourceful. Their presence always has something positive to add.

People above the life-line recognize the gifts, talents and potentials in others and admire, respect and work to benefit from them. They live to be the best they can ever be. However, while working towards their ultimate goal, they enjoy every single moment of the journey – understanding that the journey is just as important as the destination.

Anyone below this line can work to move above the line; and all those above the line, can apply themselves further both to maximize their capacity to remain above as well as improve on their placement above the line. Let the journey begin. Friends, strive to make 10 always. This is why you must scale new heights!

CHAPTER 9

LIFE IS A GIFT; LIVING IS A BUSINESS

Life is a gift, living is a business. God gave us lives, but we live the life as a business. Like all businesses, you either succeed in it, or you fail.

People succeed or fail by CHOICE. You, therefore, either choose to succeed or choose to fail. I am sure somebody is saying, but how can one choose to fail. You can choose to fail consciously or otherwise. But the end result is always the same – failure!

When you refuse to choose to succeed, you have passively chosen to fail. For instance, when you refuse divine opportunities that come your way, you have chosen to fail. When you excuse yourself from things programmed for your success, you have chosen to fail. When you see the challenges and not the opportunities in life and allow the challenges to deter you from taking steps, you have chosen to fail.

Success in life is a choice. You are the choice you make. Your career, vocation, studies, marriage, finances, can all enjoy success if you make the right choices. Show me a man who is succeeding, and you have seen a man who has made choices to succeed.

Choices! We make them every day; actually, every single minute. Today, you chose what you wore, whether to go to work or not, whether to pray or not, whether to stay indoors because of the rain or dare the rain and go to work, who to marry, where to work, when to eat, when to sleep, what to do with your spare time, etc. We make choices every minute of every day. It is the cumulative effects of these choices that determine whether we succeed in life or not.

Friends, life is a gift. You did not decide to be born, who your parents should be, when and where you were born or even your sex (male or female). You did not decide the colour of your hair, eyes, skin, height, genotype, and even your tribe or country. Life is a gift.

But living is a business. And like every business, you succeed or fail by choice. You decide what you do with life. Life is like an egg. You can eat it, throw it away, allow it to get rotten, or turn it into an omelette. Life is a gift, living is a business.

You can choose how your life will go, what you want to become, where you want to live and how you want your life to end.

The, Bible speaking about a young man called Jotham said, "Jotham became mighty because he prepared his way..."(2 Chronicles 27:6). Choice. For every mighty man, woman, organization, family, there is always a "because". For instance, "he passed his examinations because he... ";"he succeeded in marriage because he....";"he became rich because....";"he lived a long life because...";, "he was the best because...";"he won the prize because..."; etc., etc. You can add the second segment to the sentences – there is always a "because" to every life events.

There is also always a "because" in every failure story – he failed his examination because...; he divorced his wife because...; he never kept a job because...; he was sacked from his place of work because...; he never married because...; he missed the appointment because...; etc., etc.

You see, there is always a **because** in all stories of life – success or failure. Why? Life is a gift, living is a business.

You are here today because you have the gift of life, but you made the choice to read this book, join a meeting, be part of a movement, attend a seminar, or even listen to a message. Therefore, at all times, you are enjoying the gift of life and the choices you have made and are making.

The truth is that you can do nothing about life as a gift (except you want to end it – but that again is part of the choice of living), but you can do everything about how you live the life you were given – and that is where choice becomes very important.

You must understand the business dimension of living. Do you want to be happy? Make the choice and see it as a business. Do you want to succeed financially, lose weight, accelerate your career, build a business, etc, see them as businesses and understand that your choice will either result in success or failure.

Delay is not only dangerous, it is deadly. Procrastination is a robber of destiny. Waiting is wasting. Blaming others is stupidity. Hoping that manna will fall from heaven and a lost uncle will leave his wealth behind for you is foolishness. Planning to kill your parents to inherit their wealth is madness. Friends, make the right choices.

Enjoy the gift of life, but see life as business and operationalize it. There are many world changers who will die as riffraff because they lack this understanding. There are many trail blazers, pathfinders and innovators whose lives will not matter because they lack this understanding. You have the privilege to read this today, maximize it now and scale new heights.

How can you maximize your life as a business? Let me share briefly the **SCOPE model**. As a noun, **scope** is defined as "the extent of the area or subject that something deals with or to which it is relevant." It can also be defined as "the opportunity or possibility to do or deal with something"

But as a verb, it means to "assess or investigate something" and to "look at carefully; to scan." In the context of this model, both the noun and verb meanings are very relevant, as we defined the extent of life and living that is relevant and have the opportunity to not only deal with living, but produce outcomes that we are and should be proud of. In addition, as a verb, the Scope Model allows us to assess and investigate our lives and living outcomes by carefully looking at what we have done, failed to do, and decide to continue or make paradigm shifts. We must also scan our environment looking at others who have succeeded or failed, and learn from their experiences to appropriate what worked for them, and avoid their mistakes. I want to believe that this Model will move you to your next level in life.

1. **STOP**: Stop doing everything you are currently doing that is not adding to your life. For instance, stop thinking negative thoughts, stop rationalizing your failures and mistakes, stop giving excuses for your inadequacies, stop the blame game, and stop destroying your life through bad habits and attitudes. Stop the negative narratives in your life. I should also add, stop envying those who are succeeding, stop laughing at those who are failing, stop using people as your yard stick for success or happiness, stop depending on people, stop running your life without a goal or target. Stop that relationship that is not adding to your life. Stop and think!

2. **CREATE**: Create a new vision, goal and target for your life. If you had some before that you are yet to implement, recreate them and make them new. There is power in new things and new moves. Rewrite the narrative in your life. Consciously make decisions that will move you forward. Consciously create a new page, chapter or book of your life. As living is a business, create a new track for your life – leave the past and focus on the future. You cannot change the past (no matter how bad or ugly

it was), but you can use today to create the future you desire. Focus on creating what you will be proud of, what you can share with your children and grandchildren, and what you can export to others. Create the life you want.

3. **OPERATIONALIZE**: Operationalize your vision, goal and target by *documenting* your thoughts, *designing* how to implement them, *developing* your plans and procedures, and *deploying* your strategies. Develop your life plans. Friends, it is never too late to start. Some may start early, some very late; but please start. The owner of Facebook started early and that of KFC started late, but both ended up as millionaires – fulfilled and very renowned. Just start. Operationalize your dreams and make them real. Begin to live your dream. The time is now.

4. **PROGRAMMING**: Program to succeed. Use the project management approach to ensure you succeed as you document your thoughts (*ensure you are time sensitive*); design (*ensure your designs are implementable and rides on current technologies and discoveries*); develop (*ensure that your products are effective and efficient*): and deploy (*ensure that you use the right strategies*). Always build in the SMART concept in all you do. Make living and your activities Simple, Measurable, Attainable, Realistic and Time Bound.

5. **EXAMINE**: Examine your progress and processes. Add milestones that will keep you on the go. Have targets that you must meet at defined points in the journey of life – and examine periodically to see if they were achieved; and if not – why not? Watch out

to ensure that you are within tolerance at all times. As it is better and cheaper to make corrections before you completely derail than wait to make massive changes at the end. Examine your decisions, your steps, your results, and your products. Examine why you succeeded or why you failed.

Life is a gift. Living is a business. Like all businesses, your success or failure in living is a choice. Make the right decisions and choices today, and maximize this gift for quality outcomes and impacts. You are blessed.

CHAPTER 10

THE DIVINE MANDATE

Here this awesome fact

¹⁴ Ye are the light of the world. A city that is set on a hill cannot be hid.¹⁵ Neither do men light a candle, and put it under a bushel, but on a candlestick; and it giveth light unto all that are in the house.¹⁶ Let your light so shine before men, that they may see your good works, and glorify your Father which is in heaven. Matthew 5:14

How do you feel knowing that the bible says you are the light of the world? It does not say "you will be, or you may be" it says, "*you are* the light of the world". Irrespective of what you think you are, you are the light. The truth is that, irrespective of how you feel or not, someone somewhere is seeing better and living better because of your light. That is why your life is not just about you, but about the people around you – your friends, family, colleagues, and associates. People are watching you and want to be like you. People see you as a model. Whether you know it or not, someone in your place of work, at home, or in the church consciously or unconsciously wants to be like you. People dress, walk, think, and eat just to be like you! Why? because you are a light. Tall or short, fat or slim, big or small, you are a light. Children look up to us, adults look unto us, because we are lights.

The Bible says, a city that is set upon a hill cannot be hidden. Whether you like it or not, even if you do not want to, you have no choice, you cannot hide. That is the divine mandate, you are created not as darkness but as light.

People's destinies are linked to your light. Light is very powerful. It has the tendency of attracting people, making you relevant in life, distinguishing you. The Bible says you are a light. It is one thing to be a light, it is another thing to maximize that light. How, Therefore, can we maximize the light in us?

1. **Make the right choices**: The choice you make, determines the next step you take. The choice you made yesterday is responsible for where you are today and the ones you will make today will determine where you will be tomorrow. Every time you make a choice, you either fan your light or quench it. Choice is a fundamental part of life. Only those that make the right choices, shine brighter. Do not be deceived by the saying "my choice is my choice" Your choice affects people. For instance, the choice on who to marry goes ahead to determine the nature, colour and behaviour of the children you would give birth to. This decision even affects generations yet unborn.

2. **Fuel Your life:** Fuel your life spiritually, physically, emotionally, socially, economically, and in all aspects of life. Fuel your life with God's word, fuel your life by reading good books, fuel your life with good food, and fuel your life with good friends. At every point in time, make a conscious effort to surround yourself with good things. Consciously take care of yourself.

3. **Be in the right Company**: Some people will do everything possible to quench your light. They will try to hide you, or shield you so that your light is not seen by others. They may do anything possible to douse it. Others will fan your light to brighten it. Anyone that is not adding to your light is subtracting from it. There is no one that comes into your life and is neutral - they either add or subtract from you. Be it in the church or in the office, in your family, please be in the right company. It is dangerous to think everyone in church is a good person. There are so many people in church that are devil's friends. Be in the right company. This also means you should not be alone because if you are alone, then your fire will go off very quickly because there will be no one around you to help fan it.

Friends you have a divine mandate to be the light. Let others draw, learn, and see better from your light. Do not be selfish with your light; share it. A candle does not lose anything by lighting others. Share your light. Be willing to light other destinies on a regular basis because by so doing your light will never quench and even if it does, there will be someone there to light you up. This is how to scale new heights!

CHAPTER 11

ENEMIES OF DESTINY

There are enemies of destiny. These enemies are seen all around us, working tirelessly to stop us from fulfilling our destinies. Understanding these enemies will help us fight them, avoid them, flee from them, and overcome them. However, it is crucial to understand that there are two classes of enemies of destiny – **the external and internal enemies.**

External Enemies of Destiny: A short look at external enemies shows the devil and his agents at work. External enemies include people who have vowed never to see us succeed; witches who have sleepless nights just to work against our success, demons and principalities sent by Satan against us and our families, and even family members who are agents of wickedness against our destiny. These external enemies manifest as sicknesses, curses, invisible obstacles/barriers, and even untimely deaths. It is our responsibility to fight these external enemies of destiny through righteousness and reliance on God and God's word.

Paul, understanding these challenges, asked that we fight the good fight of faith (1 Timothy 6:12). This is a battle that we MUST fight. Unless we fight for our destinies, we will die as losers. Only the overcomers make it to the throne of glory, the place of beauty and the sure dwelling places of life. We overcome external enemies of destiny to scale new heights.

Internal Enemies of Destiny: This second type of enemies – the internal enemies – are never spoken about, especially in most churches and ministries. They are hardly ever discussed. Everyone is after the external enemies, but no one seems to talk about these internal enemies. These enemies are seen in all areas of our lives, but I will again limit my discussion as I shall only be looking at three verses of the Bible:

Isaiah 47:7-10:*[7] **And thou saidst, I shall be a lady for ever: so that thou didst not lay these things to thy heart, neither didst remember the latter end of it.[8] Therefore hear now this, thou that art given to pleasures, that dwellest carelessly, that sayest in thine heart, I am, and none else beside me; I shall not sit as a widow, neither shall I know the loss of children:...[10] For thou hast trusted in thy wickedness: thou hast said, None seeth me. Thy wisdom and thy knowledge, it hath perverted thee; and thou hast said in thine heart, I am, and none else beside me.***

From the above scriptures, what are these internal enemies of destiny?

1. **Self-Assurance** *(Vs 7 – And thou saidst, I shall be a lady for ever:...).* Self-assurance is one of the greatest enemies of destiny. The Bible said that, "...by strength shall no man prevail (1 Samuel 2:9), "...for without me ye can do nothing" (John 15:5); "...not by might, not by power...."(Zechariah 4:6) and "...the race is not to the swift, nor the battle to the strong, neither yet bread to the wise, nor yet riches to men of understanding, nor yet favour to men of skill..." (Ecclesiastes 9:11). When we depend on our qualifications, our connections with men, our strengths, our backgrounds, our parents, our experiences, our beauty or our past successes, we are programming for eternal failure. Self-assurance is a major internal enemy of destiny.

2. **Forgetfulness of divine interventions** *(Vs 7 - so that thou didst not lay these things to thy heart, neither didst remember the latter end of it).* Whenever we live in forgetfulness, we program ourselves to fail. It is always easy to forget the things that God has done for us when we face new life challenges; easy to murmur and complain rather than recalling God's marvellous works in our lives and career. When we forget HIS acts, we make HIM forget our current needs and future desires. Whenever we fail to regard the works of the Lord, nor the operations of HIS hands, He promises to destroy us and not build us up (Psalm 28:5). Forgetfulness of HIS acts and miracles makes God our enemy. And when we have God as our enemy, dear, we truly have an obstacle.

3. **Careless living** *(Vs 8 ...)" thou that art given to pleasures, that dwellest carelessly")*. Careless living destroys destinies. Majority live carelessly with their body, their resources, their words, their career, their marriages, their health, etc. They go everywhere, eat everything, associate with everybody, attend every program, buy everything, sleep everywhere, etc. When we lack control of what we do, we also lose control of our destiny. When we run from a fight, we meet the fight in the future. When we spend our time doing what we ought not to be doing, we miss what we ought to be doing. Great destinies are destroyed by careless living. The more careless one is, the more curses he/she accumulates on periodic basis. A major source of carelessness is the desire for pleasures...when we are given to pleasures, we may end up becoming victims of carelessness.

4. **Pride** (Vs 8:"*...that sayest in thine heart, I am, and none else beside me")*. Pride is a major enemy of destiny. It destroys lives. Thus, God will say, "Pride goeth before destruction, and a haughty spirit before a fall" (Proverbs 16:18). Furthermore, the Scripture says, "God resisteth the proud..." (James 4:6, 1 Peter 5:5). Pride again makes God a resistor to our growth, advancement and progress. Pride is a major internal enemy of destiny. According to 1John 2:16, the pride of life – like lust of the eyes and flesh - are not of God and, therefore,destroys destinies.

5. **Self-dependence (Vs: 8 "**...*that sayest in thine heart, I am, and none else beside me")*. Everyone needs someone else. God worked as a team

(Trinity) in Genesis Chapter 1; Jesus had the 12, 72 and 120 followers; and the Apostles were sent out two by two. It is dangerous to be alone. Thus, the Holy Scriptures has this to say,

"Two are better than one; because they have a good reward for their labour.[10] For if they fall, the one will lift up his fellow: but woe to him that is alone when he falleth; for he hath not another to help him up.[11] Again, if two lie together, then they have heat: but how can one be warm alone? [12] And if one prevail against him, two shall withstand him; and a threefold cord is not quickly broken." (Ecclesiastes 4:9-12);

Also, Proverbs said,*"[17] Iron sharpeneth iron; so a man sharpeneth the countenance of his friend."* (Proverbs 27:17); and *"[20] He that walketh with wise men shall be wise: but a companion of fools shall be destroyed."*(Proverbs 13:20).

Walking alone in life is self-destructive as there is no self-made man. We cannot also do all things, be in several places at the same time, solve all personal problems and meet all our needs. We need people around us. No matter how gifted a man is, he cannot get pregnant. That is why the all wise GOD informed us all that it is not wise or good for a man to be alone (Genesis 2:18). Self-dependency is a major enemy of destiny.

6. **Reliance on the wisdom of this world** (Vs 10 *"For thou hast trusted in thy wickedness: thou hast said, none seeth me. Thy wisdom and thy knowledge, it hath perverted thee")*. God sees the wisdom of

men as wickedness andtherefore as enemy of destiny. Also, when we personally get involved in wickedness, depend on diabolic means, charms and amulets; do wickedness to meet our heart desires and even go out of our ways to do what is wrong; we are most commonly working against our own destinies.

According to the same chapter of the scriptures in verses 9 and 11, these internal enemies lead to instant devastation and destruction. Hear the prophet again,

"⁹ But these two things shall come to thee in a moment in one day, the loss of children, and widowhood: they shall come upon thee in their perfection for the multitude of thy sorceries, and for the great abundance of thine enchantments....¹¹ Therefore shall evil come upon thee; thou shalt not know from whence it riseth: and mischief shall fall upon thee; thou shalt not be able to put it off: and desolation shall come upon thee suddenly, which thou shalt not know."

Since our God, is our judge, our lawgiver, and our king and is committed to saving us (Isaiah 33:22), He has also designed and developed a way out of these internal enemies of destiny. He therefore has this to say in Hebrews 2:1 *"Therefore we ought to give the more earnest heed to the things which we have heard, lest at any time we should let them slip."*

We need to take MORE EARNEST HEED to the things which we hear daily so as to avoid slipping in destiny. To this end

1. We must take more earnest heed to the WORD of instructions and ensure that they do not slip out of our mind and soul to avoid a slippery destiny.
2. We must take a more earnest heed of the words that we hear from the world and destroy them before they destroy us.
3. We must take a more earnest heed of the things we listen to and hear as they may cause our destiny to slip from us.

Let us together fight the good fight as we war against both external and internal enemies of destiny. This is a must to scale new heights.

CHAPTER 12

SECURING YOUR TOMORROW

Let me begin by stating that things happen – and majority of them are not good. Things happen to us so unexpectedly that unless we plan and prepare for them, we may not recover from them. Similarly, opportunities come our way – only the prepared and ready will be able to explore and maximize them.

Once upon a time, a father was old and about to die. He wanted to bless his son before dying. So he made a single request, "get me food to eat and I will have the strength to bless you." This was all he asked. But the events that unfolded will amaze you. While the person who was asked to get the food went to the 'bush' in search of what to prepare, the unqualified took from his savings and prepared a delicious meal for his father. Now hear what his father had to say;

20 And Isaac said unto his son, how is it that thou hast found it so quickly, my son? And he said, Because the Lord *thy God brought it to me.* Genesis 27:20

Did Jacob speak the whole truth to his father? No. He played a significant role in that process. Every time we talk about the young man Esau, how he lost his birth right, his blessing and all, we never ask ourselves; why did he really lose his birth right? Why did he lose his blessings? Was it because of Jacob, Rebecca, or Isaac? No. He lost it the first time when he said to Jacob "give me porridge that I may eat, what is this birth right all about?" His desire for an immediate gratification cost him his birth right.

To him, the birth right was useless. He had no vision. To him what he could get right now was more important than what tomorrow will serve him. For a plate of pottage of yam, he despised his tomorrow. Like Esau, many of us live a life of now and never think of tomorrow. Change, to scale new heights!

Again, when it was time for him to be blessed by his father, his father pretended like he didn't know he had sold his birth right and tried to reinstate him as his first son. He wanted to give him the blessings of a father like Abraham did. But again, he failed and lost it to Jacob. Friends, you must deliberately work to secure your tomorrow.

Esau was a very hard-working man. He would go to the bush, kill animals, but will eat everything. Anytime he needs more meat, he goes back to the bush. Jacob on the other hand reared animals in the house. He always had savings. At the hour of blessings, while Esau was in the bush looking for another animal to kill, Jacob took from what he had, dressed it, brought it to the father and the father blessed him.

How does this apply to us as individuals? If all you earn every month finishes before the end of the month, you are an Esau. I don't care how much you earn. If you have no savings or investments from your monthly income, you are an Esau. Esau did not lose his blessings because of Jacob; he did because he had no plans for the future.

My counsel is this: Every year have a project in mind that you must execute, have a target you must achieve otherwise you will be a terrible Esau. To me, Esau sounds like 'eyesore'. Do not be an eyesore in your career, destiny, and family.

At the end of the month, when you get paid, do not go to a mall and begin to shop for unnecessary things. The truth is most of the things you buy are not needed. Some of the new clothes and shoes are never worn again after a month! Friends, if you have one million dollars and you take away one dollar from it, you are no longer a millionaire. If you have Ten thousand dollars and you take away one dollar, you now have nine thousand plus.

How can you avoid being an Esau?

1. **Plan for the future, your destiny and your career:** Nothing good happens on its own. Most things that happen on their own are negative things. Plan and program yourself for the next level, phase and assignment. Imagine you lose your job for the next 6 months, how will you survive? If you have one million and you spend it all in buying a car, then you are not planning because that car will need maintenance and fuelling. Woe betides you if that

car gets stolen or it's involved in an accident; then you are back to square one. Plan!!!

2. **Do a risk assessment at all times:** Rich men take risks, but not any kind of risks. They take reasonable risks. I have a friend who worked with us for a while, got a job offer and then moved to this new organization, it looked like it was a really good move but a few months later, he got another job offer with higher pay and moved again. Few months later, the new project ended and now he is in the job market. Job or no job, he has bills to pay. Do a proper risk assessment. Not all that glitters, we are told, is gold. Do a risk assessment for every step you take. Understand that you are free to make any decision in life, but you are not free to determine the consequence of that decision.

3. **Break the Parkinson's law:** *The Parkinson's law states that everyone tends to spend all that he/ she makes every month and slightly more.* Your expenditures are in tandem with your income. No one ever becomes financially buoyant living under that law. You must consciously break it otherwise you would die in penury. When I was making $22,000 a month, I said to myself, "if I earn $40,000, I would save $20,000. Friends that never happened! If you do not consciously break this law, it would destroy you. Get out of the Esau's paradigm by breaking this law. Every month ask yourself; "what have I achieved with the money I have?" If all you do is wake up, go to work, buy food and pay rent then you are of all men most miserable.

There are things you should not be doing at 50 - like paying house rent. When I came across Parkinson's law a few years back, I said to myself I must break it; and friends, everything you see around me today speaks to my success in breaking the law.

Have a tangible and deliberate yearly project you must embark on. Plan your life, family, destiny and future as planning secures your tomorrow. Today was yesterday's tomorrow. When I was 20 years, I had many things planned out to achieve at 40 because I thought 40 would never come. Today friends I'm far over 40. If you think tomorrow will never come, you are deceiving yourself. It will creep upon you as a thief in the night; and overtake you.

Secure your tomorrow and scale new heights.

CHAPTER 13

THERE IS MORE IN YOU

Job 36:26; 37:5

²⁶ Behold, God is great, and we know him not, neither can the number of his years be searched out. ⁵ God thundereth marvellously with his voice; great things doeth he, which we cannot comprehend.

We serve a great God. He doeth great things. Why? Only a great God can do great things. No other god can claim to be great – except Jehovah! He is great and my little boy – Winner - says, "every single thing about our God is great." I completely agree with him. You were created by the great God. You are a child (if you are born-again) of this great God. You cannot but be great because "great things doeth he, which we cannot comprehend." That is why I want to share with you on *"There is more in you"*

Please understand that God has promised to bless them that fear Him, both small and great… and to increase you more and more, you and your children (Psalm 115: 13 – 15). No matter where you are right now, with God, there is what he calls more. God has not stopped working on us nor blessing us. God has not stopped increasing us. He says I will increase you more and more, both the big ones and the small ones; both great and small. So, if you are up already, there is a place called more; and if you are down; there is a place called up. How much more is God promising us today?

Deuteronomy 1: 11 answered this very important question. God promises from the scripture to "…*make you a thousand times so many more as ye are, and bless you, as he hath promised you*!" What a promise! I mean 1000 times your present capacity now. If you are earning a N1000.00, God said He has the capacity to turn this into a N1,000,000.00. If you make 10,000 per month, God said you will begin to earn N10 million per month. Just imagine it. This must be why Bishop David Oyedepo said, "if you do not break the current record in your area of calling, you have not yet succeeded. And if you do not break your father's record, you are a failure." Why? Because God says, "*I will make you a thousand so many more…*" If God says He will do it, He has the capacity to do it and He will do it. So, if your life's goal is to be as your father, you are already a failure!

To Him, *A little one shall become a thousand, and a small one a strong nation: I the LORD will hasten it in his time*(Isaiah 60:22). This means that even the little ones can become a thousand times more. God is willing, God is able, and God is capable of doing it. But, are you ready to access the *more and more* blessings that God has in stock for you? Friends, there is more in you. For you to get to the place where God has prepared for you, these 7 'Rs' are critical

1. **Realize: *You must realize that where you are, is not your final destination***. No, it is not your end point. You are still on a journey. You are a work in progress (WIP). Realize that the day you think you have arrived, you have begun to fail. Success is not a destination, but a walk. Success is defined as continuous improvement from where you are. If you end this year where you began the New Year, you have not made any progress. There must be that realization that you have to move forward in life. Realize that there are greater mountains to conquer. To conquer these new mountains, you must...

2. **Refuse: *You must refuse the Status Quo***. People tend to stay in their comfort zones and believe in "what shall be shall be". Where you are, is never a destination. Refuse the status quo and forge ahead. Refuse that things don't work in your environment, occupation, industry or family. Refuse the analysis of the national economy, systems and development. Refuse that there are no jobs and no money. Remember that people are still building houses, making millions, employing workers, and buying cars. Refuse that you cannot move forward. Refuse to stay at the same spot. Refuse stagnation and move forward to the next level. However, to move forward, you must...

3. **Release: *You must release your faith and potentials.*** Never limit yourself to where you are, but release your faith and potentials. Believe in

yourself. Believe that you can do it. Believe that you can make a difference. Believe in your God and in your dreams. Release your faith. Fate is not real,but faith works. Recall that without faith, you cannot please God (Hebrews 11:6). You need faith to make a mark. The greater the faith, the more the impact. Therefore, release your faith. See beyond where you are today, look from where you are and see beyond your present circumstances. See yourself making global impacts, touching lives, changing people and things, becoming the agent of positive social change. Release your faith! Remember that until it is bigger than you, God may not be needed. Seek dreams that are bigger than you – Big Hairy Audacious Goals (BHAC). Release your faith. But to effectively pursue your faith, you must...

4. **Return: *You must return from all prodigal journeys.*** If you have gone astray, made mistakes, or taken wrong steps, you must return. Several times we feel too proud to say I am sorry or to turn back. So, we continue on the wrong path. This destroys our destinies. You must return. If you are in a wrong relationship, just return; if you have taken trillions of steps on the wrong direction, please return. Why? because you cannot get to where God has prepared for you following the wrong path. No matter how long you fast and pray, if you are on a wrong track and choose to remain there, you can never arrive at your destination. If you have chosen to do wrong, return; if you have chosen to tell lies, return; if you have chosen to cheat, return. Many of us have to return from things that are not valuable to our life,

and that cannot get us to our destiny. Once you have returned, then you must...

5. **Resist: *You must resist every discouragement*.** You must resist mediocrity, average existence, failures and nay-sayers. Some people are so comfortable being mediocre in life. Some will say, "As long as I get my daily pay every month, as long as I am able to feed myself every month, as long as I can summit my report every week, I am ok." Resist mediocrity. Ask yourself every day, every week, or every month, "What additional value am I adding to my life and my organization?" Resist mediocrity and every discouragement. People may ask you, "Are you the only one? Are you the only staff in the organization? Are you the only one in that family?" Resist every discouragement. In life, there are **refreshers, refiners, reflectors, reducers and rejecters** according to John Maxwell. Go for only refreshers and refiners and resist the rest. To succeed in this, you must...

6. **Respect: *You must respect laws, codes and rules.*** Don't break the rules. Stay within the defined boundaries. Don't say because you want to achieve results quick, you must break the laws and rules. Don't say because others are breaking the rules, you too must break them. Respect the standard, respect your work Standard Operating Procedures, respect the codes and guidelines. Why? because if you break the laws, the law will also break you. Finally, and most importantly, you must...

7. **Relax: You must relax in God and enjoy the fruits of your labour.** Relax on His promises and

faithfulness. Relax on His Word. Yes, things may get tough, but then you must relax on Him who knows tomorrow, sees tomorrow and knows the destination. He promised to guide and lead you, therefore relax on Him. Be anxious for nothing... just relax on HIM!

Friends, just relax on God. These are the 7Rs that will move you from where you are to where God is taking you to. Remember, there is so much more in you.

When you maximize these 7Rs – Realize, Refuse, Release, Return, Resist, Respect, and Relax; you begin to enjoy the following outcomes; **Rest** (from poverty and ill-health), **Returns** (on your investment and seeds sown), **Rewards** (from God and men), **Respect** (from friends and family), and amazing **Resources** (financial and material resources towards better health, success and significance).

CHAPTER 14

MISSING LIFE'S OPPORTUNITIES

Job 31: 40; 32: 1

⁴⁰ Then let thistles grow instead of wheat, and weeds instead of barley." The words of Job are ended. ¹ So these three men ceased answering Job, because he was righteous in his own eyes.

The words of job were ended, and the three men ceased to answer because Job was complete and perfect in his own eyes. He was righteous in his own eyes! He did not need any help any more. According to him, he did not need any guidance.

In life, one of the greatest opportunities we enjoy is counselling and mentorship. *Bible says in the multitude of counsellors there is safety* (Proverb 11:14). When you get to a point in life when nobody can talk to you, advise or guide you, you are on the path to destruction. When you get to a point, whereby you know it all and every other person around you is ignorant, you have missed it. No matter where you are in life, counsel and mentorship are critical. I normally say to people that everything can be improved upon, including the very best. This is because, yesterday's best is today's obsolete; and today's best, is tomorrows useless. Remember Peugeot 404, 504, and 505 of the 80s and 90s? Today, nobody buys them anymore. They were the best of those days, but useless today. Remember Nokia 3310? Remember Thuraya? When Kodak refused to improve, they lost the market share!

Certificate gives power to learn but it does not give skills. You cannot say because you graduated with a first class that you know it all. One of the best rules of life is the rule of opportunity and mentorship. Many of us close our minds to advice and mentorship and so deny ourselves these golden opportunities of life. Our reference verses say that *Job was so righteous in his own eyes, so nobody could talk to him anymore*! How many times have people who have your best interests stopped speaking to you about issues because you are so sure of yourself and seem to know it all? A life that can never be changed is a life programmed for destruction. Why? Because great men change their minds. The only person that does not change is God. But even God changed His mind. When we call God "the unchangeable changer" it does not include His mind – God changes His mind and plans. For instance, God was once so furious against the Israelites that He said;

⁹ *I have seen these people, …and they are a stiff-necked people.* ¹⁰ *Now leave me alone so that my anger may burn against them and that I may destroy them. Then I will make you into a great nation. (Exodus 32:9-10)*

But Moses reasoned with God and God changed His mind(Exodus 32:11-14). If God could listen to mortal men and heed to their advice, you are killing yourself by not listening to the counsel of wise men!

Moses saw God face to face. He is the only man that ever saw God face to face and lived. But while leading the 3 million people, he was doing everything by himself, and was both stressing the people and himself until his father-in-law (Jethro), who never attended any school, and did not know about the Jewish traditions came to his rescue through a timely management advice. Moses was amazed at this wisdom and changed his management style. Moses was therefore able to live up to 120 years with good vision and strength just because he listened and harkened to an old man's counsel (Deuteronomy 34:7). He accepted mentorship.

Joshua had no family we know about in the Bible, but followed Moses, and later took over from Moses. He became the one that led Israel into the Canaan land. The biggest opportunities in life are in the place of mentorship and counselling. Friend! Don't block yourself away from life's opportunity.

Friends, you can learn from anybody – including a mad man on the street as most great discoveries on earth happened accidentally. Newton's law of gravity, law of floatation, etc., were all accidental discoveries. Do not close your mind to information or knowledge; you will not be hurting any other person but yourself. Remember that although multitude of years should teach wisdom, **Great men are not *always* wise,** nor do the aged *always* understand justice (Verse 7 – 9).

Job's friends left him alone because he had all the answers. Job's suffering may have reduced from 41 chapters to less than 5 chapters if he listened to wise counsel. Similarly, our lives challenges do not need to last for decades. Listen to counsel and accept to be mentored. This accelerates our journey to new heights.

CHAPTER 15

PATHWAY TO PROMOTIONS

In life we all desire to be promoted. We wish it, we pray for it, we hope that somebody ahead of us will leave so we take over their place. We pray, wish and hope for promotions in everything. Although praying for promotion is good, there is a divine pathway to promotion. It is important for us to understand that one's number of years does not equal to promotion. In life, promotions are not given, they are merited. If promotion is your desire in any area of life, then pay attention to this bible passage;

Exodus 36: 1 & 2: *Then wrought Bezaleel and Aholiab, and every wise hearted man, in whom the Lord put wisdom and understanding to know how to work all manner of work for the service of the sanctuary, according to all that the Lord had commanded.*

2 And Moses called Bezaleel and Aholiab, and every wise hearted man, in whose heart the Lord had put wisdom, even every one whose heart stirred him up to come unto the work to do it:

Understand that only those who are wise hearted are qualified for promotion. While others are complaining and murmuring, those who are wise hearted are discovering their gifts, talents and skills and applying them for exploits. First Bezaleel and Aholiab worked for free using their God given talents and skills, then Moses called them and gave them a higher assignment.

It is self-deception and self-illusion to fold your hands and think that somebody will come one day, find you, and give you a job or promote you to the next level. In the book of Matthew 25:15, the Bible talks about a certain man travelling into a far country who delivered unto his servants' talents according to their different abilities.

15 And unto one he gave five talents, to another two, and to another one; to every man according to his ability; and straightway took his journey.

God has given you and I gifts, and talents called wisdom, understanding, and skills. He has given you and me certain privileges that no one else has. It is your application and engagement with these talents and gifts that qualifies you for promotions. Take for instance, you are given a job as logistic officer and you have skills on ICT or on other aspect and say because I have not been paid for this work then I will hide my skills. You not only deny yourself promotions, you also deny yourself a chance to get better at what you do. Every skill, capacity or wisdom you have is for exploits; and in science whatever you don't use, you lose. So unused skills decrease in value and become useless with time.

When I was working with US Centers for Disease Control and Prevention, Nigeria, I was employed as a Networks Coordinator. My Job Description was to organize the system, network funders, implement partners and service delivery points. However, when I discovered a gap in OVC program, I volunteered to help out. I combined OVC services with my primary assignment - Networking. That was where I learned how to produce guidelines, strategic documents, and several other skills I am using today. Bezaleel and Aholiab did the work first before they were found by Moses and promoted. And because they chose to work with their minds, verse 3 became a reality:

3 And they received of Moses all the offering, which the children of Israel had brought for the work of the service of the sanctuary, to make it withal. And they brought yet unto him free offerings every morning.

When your skill is in use, resources follow! When skills and talents are exploited, contract and grants become reality. *If you are just working to make money, you will die in poverty*; *and if you are working for what you will get from the work you will die in frustration*. This is because, there is no amount a company can pay you that will satisfy your needs. I don't do things because of money; I do things because I have the skill to do them.

If what you want is promotions, then maximize your skill, maximize the wisdom and gifts of God in your life. Don't side-line yourself to one single area and say "this is my calling, this is what I have being paid for and this is what I will do", then you will end up denying yourself privileges and promotions. Bezaleel and Aholiab worked, and Moses found them and promoted them.

Learn to volunteer with your skills and talents. Learn to occupy with your skills. Learn to enhance your relevance with your talent and gift that God has given to you. There is nobody who does not have unique gifts, unique talents and unique callings. Everyone has something unique that will make them stand out. But if you don't identify it and utilize it, you deny yourself of getting the benefit linked to it. By applying yourself where you are now, and maximizing the gift and calling of God in your life, your life will make a difference in the precious name of Jesus.

CHAPTER 16

DANGERS OF NOT APPLYING YOURSELF

Job 15:31: *³¹ Let not him that is deceived trust in vanity: for vanity shall be his recompense.*

If you think you are deceiving anybody, that is not true. If you say I have been able to deceive them with my way of living; I have been able to deceive them with my attitude, I have been able to deceive them with my composure; the Bible says that vanity shall be your ultimate reward! You do not need to pray, or trust it; it will just come and in very large quantity. Vanity – nothingness!

Also, Verse 34 says; *³⁴ **For the congregation of hypocrites shall be desolate, and fire shall consume the tabernacles of bribery.***

Living a hypocritical life results in desolation. If before people you are an angel, but when you are alone you are a devil – you are a hypocrite. And the Bible says that desolation awaits you. Understand that you are not working for anybody, but primarily for yourself. As long as your conscience does not judge you, you are not under any condemnation.

Deceivers will inherit vanity and hypocrites will have destruction in large quantity. Who are the deceivers? Those who have gifts and talents but, choose to hide them or refuse to maximize them. Please, occupy your place in destiny with your talents and gifts. Decide to scale new heights with your gifts, talents and expertise.

PART 2

LIFE REALITIES

CHAPTER 17

GRATITUDE IS A CHOICE

Gratitude is not a gift from God, it is not a skill you acquire, it is not a function of what you have or have not received, nor a function of how voluminous the gift was. I have come to discover that everything that is important in life is a choice – including gratitude. Serving God, getting married, coming to work, or behaving well is a choice, almost everything that pertains to life is a choice. However, you are free to make any choice, but you are not free to determine the consequence of the choices made.

In Luke 17:11-19: Jesus healed ten lepers, but only one returned to appreciate him. He was sad and wondered where the rest were. To show that gratitude pays, He made the grateful leper whole.

If only 10% was grateful to Jesus, it is very wrong to think that everybody you help will be grateful to you. It is natural and normal for people to be ungrateful. What has become unusual is to see grateful people who are grateful all the time. This is why God expects our thanksgiving even as we expect His answers to our prayers. Similarly, a man expects our gratitude even as we make request from them.

Based on this experience of Jesus, let me elaborate here on the **Three R's of Gratitude**

1. **RECOGNIZE:** Always RECOGNIZE that someone has helped you. The leper saw (recognized) that he was healed and thus took steps to appreciate the source. Recognize that God has answered your prayers, provided your needs, responded to your request, fulfilled your expectations, and even fought your battles. Every blessing you have cost God something. The price for our salvation was his son, Jesus. As God uses people to bless us, when blessed, recognize that someone has gone out of his way to help you. Be grateful to those that God used to help you. Remember, there is NO self-made man. Every one climbs on the shoulders of others to see better – so RECOGNIZE!

2. **RETURN:** After recognizing that you have received help, **RETURN** to that person (and God) to show gratitude. The leper returned to Jesus. Return to your source and say, without any equivocation, that you are grateful. Return to whosoever helped you in career, finances, or marriage and show some gratitude. When you return to your source, like the grateful leper, your source will never run dry. If you refuse to return, you block the channel of God's blessing.

3. **RELEASE** His glory. In Luke, the leper opened his mouth and glorified God. It always pays to show your gratitude with your voice. Learn and choose to be grateful. When you are grateful, you are qualified for the best. When the leper came back to thank

Him, Jesus made him whole. The nine that did not come back were never made whole.

It means that there are certain things that are still in the hands of the source, and except you return to the source you cannot get them. Some people are happy with what they have attained. They are satisfied with just one tenth of the blessings. But there is a 9/10 in the hand of the man that gave you that gift that if only thou can be sensible enough to return, you have access to it all. Choose to be grateful to anybody and everybody who has been of help to you.

Your ingratitude can cost you more than you can ever imagine. Many things have happened around you that you do not know anything about. People make decisions on you without you knowing about them. People talk about you in places you can never visit. Be grateful to God and the man or woman God is using to advance your life. Do not say 'I thank God' only. Thank your parents, spouse, children, relations, partners, colleagues, and people that have added values to your life. You can also thank those that did wrong things to you for it made you to become who you are today. Remember "…all things worketh together for your good". Even the molestations worked for your good.

Be grateful!

CHAPTER 18

THE DANGERS OF DISCONTENTMENT

The book of Esther Chapter 5 tells a very interesting story of a married man called Haman. This Haman was the king's right-hand man and was doing well both as a politician and in family life. Actually, the King had just recently promoted him and he was the only person invited to dine with the King and his queen (vs 5 & 6). However, all these privileges and blessings did not satisfy Haman as each time he passed by the King's gate and saw Mordecai who would not bow to him, he became very bitter (vs 9). He then made up his mind to destroy the poor man. When he told his wife and friends, they advised him to dig a gallows for Modercai (vs10-14). But the Bible admonishes us that *"...godliness with contentment is great gain."(*1Timothy 6:6)

Success is not a destination as today's success is tomorrow's failure. At the pinnacle of every success achieved is a new set of challenge. If one gets a degree today, the next pursuit is to get a job. If a person gets married today, the next desire is to have a child. When a couple gets a child, they need to stay awake to nurse the baby, train and pay associated bills. This was the case with Haman. He was promoted by the king, told his friends "of the glory of his riches, and the multitude of his children, and all the things wherein the king had promoted him, and how he had advanced him above the princes and servants of the king." (V11). Yet, he wanted something else.

Friends, we ought to celebrate every stage we find ourselves. We should learn to be content with what we have per time. I met a group of ladies in a prayer meeting who were very ready to table their requests before God because they wanted children. I had to first open their eyes to the numerous blessings of God in their lives for which they ought to thank God. Sometimes, our needs blind us to the good things that God has done for us. And we end up postponing our joy and happiness without knowing that life is not a destination, but a journey.

Many people fail to enjoy their present position because they have their eyes on a position they are yet to attain. Many people lose the best of life because they concentrate on things that are yet to materialize. Some, instead of appreciating the good things God has done for them, focus on their unmet needs and wants.

Friends, do you know that every success is a doorway to another (set of) challenge(s)? Therefore, be content at every level you are. Remember that, for every stage you are in, there are so many things to thank God for. Don't allow the blindfolding of the future to make you miss the beauty of where you are. It is important to understand that

your current position is someone's prayer point. All the multibillionaires you are looking up to, from Bill Gate to Warren Buffet still have something they are believing God for. Many ladies want to be billionaire's wives, but can they marry these kind of persons; are they strong enough to be their wives?" You cannot enjoy their wealth without managing them as a person!

What are therefore the dangers of discontentment?

1. **Lost opportunities for real living:** Discontentment makes people to miss out on life. If a man enjoys his present level, when another level comes, he will be well qualified to enjoy it. You don't need to miss today that you have for the sake of tomorrow that you may never have. The only currency you have at hand is today, you may not be there tomorrow. Celebrate every day of your life as life is a gift. Have fun at the stage you are in; enjoy your work, family, resources, salary. Enjoy what you have today, don't wait till when you start earning a million before you start enjoying life. Be content where you are. Worry is the price you pay for a future you may never see. Some people get children and lose all they have. Some people even get children and they don't ever enjoy these children. Be contented!

2. **Blindness to the good in people:** Discontentment makes people not to see or celebrate the good in others. Every destiny that comes around you is there to add value to you consciously or unconsciously. If they don't add value to you, they position you for something better. People come into your life for

three reasons - as friends, enemies, or nobodies. All add value to you. Look out and see the good in all.

3. **Loss of resources and opportunities:** Discontentment makes you lose resources, talents and gifts. In a bid to get what you don't have, you lose all you have and all you have worked for. A young man like Haman with all his riches couldn't enjoy it because of discontentment. He was supposed to deploy his talents and skills to advance his life, but he was destroyed before his time.

4. **Untimely deaths:** One of the major dangers of discontentment is untimely death. People die before their time because of discontentment, as seen in the case of Haman. The irony of it is that he lost his life in the same gallows he had dug for another man because he was not satisfied with his current position.

Other consequences of discontentment are jealousy, lack of satisfaction, losing favour with people, stealing, greed, selfishness, ill health etc. People can even kill for this purpose as seen in the case of Cain and Abel. Discontentment is like a cankerworm and I pray God will save us from being destroyed by it in Jesus Name. Amen

CHAPTER 19

REMEMBER OR REGRET

Remember or regret. Two words that do not look alike but are very similar. But the good news is that you can either remember or you regret – it is all about choice!

Friends let me share with you a story from 2 Chronicles Chapter 22-24. Ahaziah, the king of Israel reigned and died. When he died, Athaliah, his mother destroyed all the sons of the king and made herself king. One child was left that was not destroyed. He was hidden in the house of Priest Jehoiada. After she had reigned for six years, the hidden son was revealed. Jehoiada gathered all the people together and made him king. At that time, he was seven years old. When Athaliah heard about it in Chapter 23, she cried, "treason, treason!!" Jehoiada ordered for her to be taken out of the house of the Lord and killed, and she was killed.

The seven-year-old boy; Joash began to reign. Jehoiada was there to support him and the bible recounts in Chapter 24 that he gave him two wives through which he had sons and daughters. In verse 15 of that chapter, Jehoiada died and they buried him in the sepulchre of the king. He wasn't a king but he was buried in the sepulchre of kings because of the life he lived. The moment he died and was buried, the established and mentored king Joash began to misbehave as he did what was not allowed nor permitted. The son of late Jehoiada, Zachariah prophesied against him. Instead of taking correction and amending his ways, Joash took offence and killed Him. The Bible records in 2Chronicles 24:22: ***Thus Joash the king remembered not the kindness which Jehoiada his father had done to him, but slew his son. And when he died, he said, The LORD look upon it, and require it.***

He remembered not the kindness that was shown to him and killed the son of the man that made him a great man.

Human beings are programmed to forget easily the kindness that people show to them. We are programmed to forget easily the good others have done to us. We are programmed to remember the things we asked for but were never given to us, and easily forget the good that was done. This is the bane of humanity. It is so easy to forget that when you were hungry, someone gave you food; when you were sick, someone visited you or paid your bills; when you were jobless, someone gave you a job; when you were homeless, someone housed you; and when you were in need, someone helped you out. It is so easy to forget those that helped you overcome life major challenges when things become comfortable for you. It is easy to trivialize the great helps rendered to you in your days of humble beginning.

I had an uncle in my village. In the 1960s, my father paid his school fees of £32 or £64. My father earned about £1:2 shillings then. In the late 80s, he came to my father with the equivalent of this amount to pay back the money my father invested in him in the 1960s. My father looked at him and rather than take offence, my father said to him, "go and do to others as I did to you". He completely forgot – that he became what he was partly by the funds my father sacrificed for him.

Do not be forgetful of the hands that lifted you from the miry clay of life. Do not think that your power and strength has done it for you. You know the truth, if there are seven staircases and someone helped you climb one, do not forget that person because that one he helped you with may be the main reason you were able to climb the other six.

My uncle remembered not. People are so good at forgetting someone who gave them a drink when they were thirsty or the person that paid their rent when they were in need. People are so good at forgetting the person who made them who they are. Friends, no one is made by himself, we are all made from people's helps.

Don't forget or you will regret. Later, in that story, enemies came and fought King Joash, the *Syrians came and waged war against him and he was very diseased.*

Verse 25: *And when they were departed from him, (for they left him in great diseases,) his own servants conspired against him for the blood of the sons of Jehoiada the priest, and slew him on his bed, and he*

died: and they buried him in the city of David, but they buried him not in the sepulchres of the kings.

His own servants conspired and killed him. The Bible says they buried him in the city of David but not in the sepulchre of the king. Jehoiada a non-king was buried in the sepulchre of kings by the seed he sowed. But Joash a king for 40 years was buried outside the sepulchre of kings because he forgot. They killed him because of the evil he did to Jehoiada and his children. The servants watched what Jehoiada did for him. They saw when Jehoiada preserved him, gave the kingdom back to him, gave him two wives through whom he had children. They were there watching how Jehoiada guided him in the affairs of life. But the moment Jehoiada died, Joash forgot. Do not forget the hands that have lifted you up. Do not burn the bridges of life.

In your village, schools, wherever you find yourselves, friends, do not be forgetful. Some have left school and need a reference, but cannot get any lecturer to stand in for them. That is very wrong. Some are working in some places but cannot ask for reference from their employers or supervisors.

We have the mentality of forgetting the people that have helped us like Joash who for this reason died a miserable death. The painful part about Joash's life is that he began very well. He collected money in abundance to rebuild the temple and rebuilt it. The moment Jehoiada died he went astray.

In your career, do not forget; in your marital life, do not forget; in your academics and spiritual life, do not forget. At every point, there is someone God has positioned in your life to make it more meaningful, do not forget them.

Even God himself does not take forgetfulness of His acts and blessing for granted. The Bible says in Psalm 28:5 that, because they regarded not the works of the Lord, nor the operations of His hands, that God will destroy them, and not build them up. So, even God gets angry when you forget him. Please do not forget God.

There is no one who has at one point in time not had a destiny helper. Friends, go back and write 10 names of people who have helped you in life and just appreciate them. No matter how little, be it a call, or a hug, just thank them. May you not be a victim of regret from deliberate or unconscious forgetfulness.

There are two common ways people express regret in life; "had I known" and "if only". These are the two most painful phrases in life. I pray for you this day that you would not be victims of such negative statements and that the grace to remain forever grateful will rest upon you in Jesus name.

CHAPTER 20

SENSITIVITY OR STUPIDITY

Everything about life is a choice and in making this choice, you are either sensitive or stupid. In the book of 1Kings 13, there is the story of a prophet who went to the kingdom of Judah to prophesy against it. After he prophesied, the king said unto him; *"come young man, stay with me and refresh thyself and I will give thee a reward"*. The man said; *"if thou will give me half thine house, I will not go in with thee neither eat bread in thy place for so was I charged by the Lord saying eat not bread nor drink not water nor turn by the way where thou comest. So he went another way different from which he entered Bethel"*.

However, if you read down to verse 11, an old prophet came and told him; *"the Lord spoke to me and asked you to follow me"*. This young man followed the prophet and went to his house and supped with him. After eating, the old prophet prophesized to him *"because you have disobeyed God, you will not get back to where you came from"* and on his way home, lions came and ate him up.

The old man then came, picked his corpse, buried him and mourned him. Was the young prophet stupid or sensitive?

In life our destinies are defined by our level of stupidity and/or sensitivity. We are either largely sensitive or we are largely stupid; highly sensitive or highly stupid. Recently, I went to a church where a guest minister preached a beautiful sermon on family life. Thereafter he called for a seed for the church and started putting oil on the palms of those that came to sow the seed. He also prophesised over them. Friends, you must be careful who prays over you, prophesizes or lays hand/legs on you or anoints you. Do you like what they carry? Do you want to be like them? Do they have a gift or story you want to have? Same thing goes for the people who go to native doctors for wealth. Most native doctors live in the forest, are very poor (or look very poor) and usually have no wife, house or anything tangible. But when he promises you the world, you believe. You do not stop and think that if this man can give you heaven and earth, why then doesn't he give same to himself first. Friends, be sensitive not stupid.

It is not every voice you hear that you should follow, it is not every news that you should listen to, it is not every prophet that should lay hands on your head, it is not every human being that should speak into your life and it is not every prayer you say amen to. Why? Because you are not a robot and serving God does not take away your brain and ability to think.

I think it was Bishop David Oyedepo who said that God gave us brains to gain so you would not be a burden to Him.

Some of us have taken Christianity to mean brainlessness and stupidity.

Friends, not everything you hear is true. In life, you are either sensitive or stupid. It is not everything that you hear that you should take into your heart and begin to apply to your life. Not every door that opens is your door of blessing. A wise man said, "all that glitters is not gold". They may look interesting and enchanting, but may not be what they look like. Friends, even Satan comes as an angel of light. As the world gets darker and darker, our sensitivity level must go higher and higher otherwise we will be victims of high level stupidity. For us who are believers we must always review all we hear to be sure they are true.

Please do not be or remain stupid, rather be sensitive. I am saying this because some people will just walk up to you, tell you a couple of stories about your past, you become mesmerized and before you know it, you give them all you ever worked for. These people may use diabolic powers. We need to be sensitive so that we do not keep falling victims of their antics. Some even use guess work. If I walk up to you and say 5 things about you, there is a probability that at least one will be correct. Just by guess work. And through body language they are able to detect the right ones.

I was once a victim of these people some years ago. I was about finishing my medical school when a lady walked up to me and said she had a vacancy in an oil firm that will fly me back and forth in a helicopter to the Off Shore Stations and with excellent pay. Friends, at that time, I had never been on a plane or helicopter, so I was very excited. I could not believe my luck. This lady took me to the interview office and was telling me how this job will change my life and move my career forward. The long and short of the story is I was scammed, and lost good money in that process.

Friends, please do not be a victim. So many people have allowed themselves to be used by the devil to commit diverse atrocities. Please, do not be one of their victims. Be sensitive. I pray God grants us understanding.

CHAPTER 21

MAXIMIZING THE TIMES AND SEASONS (MONTHS)

Time is one word everybody uses, but people hardly ever define it. We understand that definition of terms facilitates better understanding and improves communication. Realizing this need, I decided to generate a practical definition of time. I define time as "partition of life into measurable segments; which could be in seconds, minutes, hours, days, weeks, months, years, decades, centuries, and millennia or fractions or multiples of the same."

In this first segment, we shall be looking at months – how can we maximize the months to scale new heights?

Why did God divide life into segments like months? What is the essence of months and how can we maximize the month? There is this saying by Myles Monroe which says, "When the purpose of a thing is unknown, abuse is inevitable." When we fail to understand the meaning and purposes of the month, abuse of the month is inevitable. Why? Because we all need "*to number our days so that we can apply our heart to wisdom" (Psalm 90:12)*. Months are significant in God's program for our lives. When a month closes and another month begins, it is not just normal or just natural. There are both physical and spiritual significance to the month.

Revelation 22 verse 1.

And he shewed me a pure river of water of life, clear as crystal, proceeding out of the throne of God and of the Lamb.

Until they show it to you, you may never see it. The water was not hiding, the river was not hiding, it was available. But God needed to show it to John before he could see it! There are a lot of things in the scripture that you read every day, but you may never find what is imbedded in them until somebody who has access and/or the key to them reveals them to you. That is why there are Ministers of the gospel, there are Priests, Prophets, Pastors, Evangelists and there are Teachers of the Word **(Ephesians 4:11)**. You may read the Bible a million times, and still fail to see what is hidden – that is the mystery of the Word of God. It says *he shew me a pure river of water of life…*

My emphasis however, today, is on verse 2: *…was there the tree of life, which bare twelve manner of fruits; and yielded her fruit every month…*

It clearly showed us that the tree of life (which is a reflection of anybody born again and in God) bears fruits every month. Each month, there are fruits expected of you to bear. This is why women have monthly menstrual flow because naturally, they lay eggs every month– not quarterly or yearly. Any month they do not see it, they become worried if not pregnant. You must also be worried any month you have no tangible fruit.

Essence and Significance of Months

Every month is ordained from heaven for you to bear a new fruit. Every month is ordained by God to deliver something unique; a unique result, a unique product, a unique fruit, a unique dividend. No month should come and pass without you being able to say categorically and tangibly that this is what I have achieved/delivered. **That, this is the fruit of this month**, the result of this month; the dividend of the month, or my reward for the month. The world copied God and began to pay salaries every month. That is why in Nigeria and in other parts of the world salary is paid on monthly basis. Imagine not having your salary every month! Monthly salary is a dividend of the month. However, the salary is a reward for work done. If therefore there are no evidences, tangible proof for the work done, then the salary you collected was not yours. If you ask to be paid for a month when you did not produce any meaningful fruit, you are a thief as the money you are asking for does not belong to you.

For instance, if you come to work by 10.00 am and leave by 2.00 pm, but collect salary for an eight hour work day (8.00 am – 5.00pm with an hour break in-between), you are a thief. This attitude is common among several public sector workers. Salary earned at the end of the month is based on the work done. But if your work does not have any tangible fruits, you don't need to earn any salary that month. Paying you for work not done makes your employer a philanthropist and a Father-Christmas. But employers by nature are not philanthropists. They are business men/ women. They want results. They employ people for results and fruits, and they expect these fruits every month.

The 4-Dimension of Fruit Bearing

At a personal level, you can bear fruits every month. Do not limit yourself to monthly salary. There are four dimensions to bearing fruits. God expects you to bear four kinds of fruit regularly – spiritual fruits; physical fruits; financial fruits, and social fruits. These are the various areas we should bear dividends every month. You are expected to earn dividends from these four main dimensions – spiritual (e.g. souls won, kingdom investments), physical (e.g. health/ wholesomeness, exercise, pregnancies, etc.), financial (e.g. academic, idea generated, career, business, income generated, etc.), and social (e.g. family, relationships, holidays, meetings, etc.). Every month should have tangible goals that you must achieve before the end of the month. Thus, at the end of every month, you must review your productivity and assess how many of your set plans were achieved.

Do not take more than you can accommodate, or bite more than you can chew. Do not set goals that will discourage you nor those that will not bring out the best in you. Set realistic goals that may stretch you, but still very much achievable. As long as you are alive, you should be bearing fruits because in you is a tree of life. By nature, ladies bear fruits every month as they lay eggs every month. If God made it that way by nature for ladies to lay eggs every month, friends, nature, God, and employers expect the same from you – bear fruits! Take a stock of the year. There are other physical, economic, spiritual and mental fruits to produce.

Do not just go to work on Monday and go back by Friday. Have a result you want to deliver every day, week, or month. Ask yourself how many lives you want to touch, what part of your earnings will go to somebody else, and how many orphans you want to visit. Have a fruit bearing mentality! God said, "every tree that beareth fruit my father will prune so that it will deliver more, but every tree that beareth not fruit shall be cut down." (*John 15:3-5*). My prayer is that none of you will be cut down at the end of the day. We all will bear fruits on monthly basis in Jesus name.

CHAPTER 22

MAXIMIZING THE YEARS

Now that we have learned how to maximize the month through monthly fruit bearing to scale new heights, it is time to maximize the years. Every twelve months delivers a year – but there are special requirements towards maximizing the years.

In Matthew 14:20 – 32, we saw a story involving Jesus and His disciples…they ate, fed five thousand people, and left in a boat, leaving Jesus behind to disperse the crowd; Jesus, after dispersing the crowd went to the mountain to pray; then He walked on water. Peter asked him and also walked on water. Few minutes later, Peter began to sink when he saw the storms and waves, but he was saved by Jesus when he cried out. And the moment they stepped into the Boat, the storm ceased.

The wind did not cease until they had come into the ship. Whatever you are seeing now that seems contrary to your destiny is only temporary. There is a way to maximize the year and enjoy what God has packaged for us. Despite the various prophetic declarations, a year may still pass without significant changes if one does not maximize the year. Prophecies are declared so that we can take responsibilities for our own testimonies. No prophecy will happen without our practical involvement.

How Can We Maximize The Year?

1. **Dream Again:** The Bible says Jesus was walking on the sea on the fourth night and the disciples saw him. What are you seeing concerning the Year? What you cannot see, you cannot experience. What is your vision, dreams, and desires for the Year? What dreams do you have? What goals have you set? They saw him walking on water. If they did not see him, the next set of verses would not have taken place. That means their eyes were open. Beyond your physical eyes, what are your spiritual eyes telling you. Are you seeing your children, your wife, husbands, houses, cars, and/or degrees? Are you seeing a bigger, fatter and wealthier bank account? What are you seeing? New things do not happen by mistake, people program them to happen. You must see for you to experience. In both physical and spiritual environment, what are you seeing?

2. **Make Demands:** *To maximize the year, you must make demands.* They saw him walk on water, so Peter said, 'if it is you, bid me come'. You must ask questions and make demands from men and from God. Why must you ask questions? To seek clarification. The problem so many people have is because their mouths are closed. You must learn to ask questions and make demands. *"If it be you, bid*

me come". Ask God for what you want. If you want children, growth in your job or need a new job, or want to get higher income, ask for it. You will never know what you would gain until you ask.

3. **Seek challenges.** It is not documented anywhere that anybody had ever walked on water before that night – at least, not to my knowledge. But Peter dared it! Dare new things. Step out of your comfort zone. Break up your fallow grounds. Stop living and thinking in the same old ways. You will sink if you do not re-invent yourself. New season demands self-reinvention. Seek new challenges to scale new heights.

4. **Take faith-full steps.** It is better to take steps and fail, than never to step out at all. If you fail, you have learnt the wrong way of doing it. If you did not take any step at all, you might think you are on the right track, when you are not. Jesus said *'come',* and Peter obeyed and walked on water. Take that step to actualize your vision, dreams, and aspirations. If you want to make a difference in the world, take steps. If you want to have a better family life, take steps. Complaining and murmuring will only make things worse. Take faith-full steps. If you want to have children, get married; if you want to get married, take required steps. The word has gone out, if you do not take steps, it will be a wasted year.

5. **Stay focused.** No matter what was said concerning this year, there would be contrary waves, storms and distractions. There will be challenges that may want to take your eyes away from your vision, dreams and plans. But stay focused. We are all in a race,

stay focused. When Peter saw the boisterous wind, he lost focus and began to sink. Learn from him, stay focused. The Bible demands that our eyes be single to enjoy full revelation and impact (Matthew 6:22). Keep your eyes on the goal or target.

6. ***Ask for Help.*** Help is available. Do not die in silence, cry for help when in need. There are no self-made men, but helped men. Everyone you see today was helped by someone. When you are hungry, sick or distressed, cry for help. Do not try to bottle up everything and die a stupid death. When the going gets tough, cry for help. God has placed people around you in church, team members, colleague, wives, and husbands to help you. Do not feel too big to ask someone for help or seek advice. The person might not give you money, but a simple advice can be all you need to come out of that problem.

7. ***Build your capacity.*** Build your spiritual, intellectual, emotional, financial and programming capacity. Build your faith. Leave where you used to be and climb that ladder of faith. Peter sank because he had little faith. Build your faith and glow. All promises of God come with their attendant responsibilities. The storms around you are opportunities to maximize the season and build your capacity. Go out there and build your capacity.

I will see you at the top of your career, finances and destiny this season as you scale new heights.

CHAPTER 23

MAKING THE END OF THE YEAR COUNT

Most of us switch off in our minds whenever the year is about to end believing that the year is over. But friends, the year hasn't ended. Many start waiting anxiously for the 1st of January and stop chasing their dreams/goals. They switch off in their career, business, academics and ministry.

Psalm 65 vs 11: "Thou crownest the year with thy goodness; and thy paths drop fatness."

It is our responsibility to make the end of our own year count. It is our responsibility not to waste the last days to weeks of the year; it is also our responsibility to maximize the things and times that we have.

Take for instance, empowerment. Empowerment is a personal choice. Nobody can empower you without your willingness. People think empowerment is someone giving you money. This is a gift not empowerment. What empowers you are the skills and life keys that are given to you. No matter how much you are given (e.g. money, food, cloths, etc.), you will spend/use it all and be in lack again; but when you acquire skills and life keys, you can use that to multiply money endlessly.

Procrastination is the worst enemy of destiny. You can achieve a lot within the last few weeks of the year. However, many enter the season's mood – Christmas mood, holiday mood and some just wait for the year to end. However, people that wait for the year to end, waste the time they would have used to make a difference. The truth is there are many people who are alive in December, but may not see the 1st of January of the coming year. They may even have 5, 10, 20 or 40 years plans in their hearts. So, postponing your life for a time you don't have is destroying your destiny. Before the end of this year, people will still buy new cars, lay foundation for their own houses, make proposals on whom to marry, get new jobs, travel abroad, create new things, start new businesses, and also get pregnant. What are you waiting for?

Don't postpone your life till the next year, make the end of the year count. God is at work, crowning the year with his goodness and causing the path of everyone to drop fatness. For many of us who are believers, this has been our prayer point: *'Lord crown my year with your goodness and let my path drop fatness'.* This is not a bad prayer item. But the bible says; *all these things worketh God often time with man.* God will not crown it for you without your involvement. Without your mind, God can do nothing. Without your participation in that process, he won't do it. So, God is at work at the end of the year crowning the year for everyone who desires to have it with his goodness and making our paths drop fatness. But there are steps and responsibilities you must take. Every year has been ordained by God to end well as according to *Ecclesiastes 7 vs 8: "The end of a matter is better than the beginning thereof"*

Things end well when men make it end well. You must work to make it end well. It's not just a confession, it's a profession. As we work into the last weeks of the year, understand that every year will end well when we walk with God to make it end well. That's why you shouldn't go on holidays towards the end of the year, don't go to sleep, and don't postpone your life till the coming year. There are still things that can be accomplished in the few days to weeks that we have in the last months of every year. If your desires for any year have not been fulfilled, there is still time for it to be fulfilled. It took God just 6 days to make the whole earth. So, one whole month is too much for God to give you your heart desires, change your status, and change everything around you.

Don't postpone your destiny, whatever needs to be done should be done. In your work plan, what ought to be achieved should be achieved. If you are travelling for Christmas, don't close your life, don't close your career, don't close your destiny. There are still things to do. Things don't happen by chance, people make them happen. As you walk towards the end of the year, crown your own year with your expectations. There is still a lot to be accomplished.

Allow yourself to be fully involved in what is going on in your organization and in your personal live. If you are in school, do your school work. If you are running a business or someone is running your business, don't just relax. Your assignments should be fully achieved. Maximize the days you have. Let your own year end well. Let there be dropping of fats upon your paths. Let there be an unusual evidence of a crowned year for you. To encounter your major mega breakthrough, someone must push or trigger it to happen. Work to scale higher heights this end of year.

No year should be allowed to end empty but with plenty–plenty of resources, blessings, and fatness. Make the rest of the year the best of the year and scale new heights.

CHAPTER 24

OVERCOMING TO SUCCEED

To succeed, you must overcome issues and challenges in life as these are daily occurrences.

In **Revelation 21:7** it is written, **"to him that overcometh, shall inherit all things. And I will be his God and he will be my son".**

Life is full of things you must overcome to succeed. There are a lot in life that we must overcome for us to inherit all things. **Psalm 18:7 says: "lines have fallen to me in pleasant places, therefore, I have a godly heritage".** Everyone has a godly heritage, but access to the godly heritage is not free. There are things you must overcome to enjoy the heritages of life. Biblically, we have seen a lot of people who have missed their inheritances because they could not overcome certain things in life. Esau could not overcome lust for food, Reuben could not overcome lust for his father's concubine, Simeon and Levi could not overcome their anger, and Cain could not overcome jealousy, so they lost their inheritances.

Although there are inheritances for everyone, access to them is a function of what you are willing to overcome. There are things you must overcome, and they come on a daily, weekly, or monthly or even yearly basis.

How do you know that you are doing well and are able to overcome issues? You must periodically evaluate yourself or allow yourself to be evaluated. Evaluations and appraisals are not done for the sake of fulfilling all righteousness. They are critical components in our success journey. There are two kinds of appraisals:

1. Self-appraisal (informal appraisals, non-defined appraisals)
2. Official appraisals (formal appraisals, defined appraisals)

Life is a stage and one stage has to be completed before starting another. Appraisals of people are done quarterly, semi-annually or yearly in organizations according to the organization's policies. Appraisals are critical to one's next level, so if your appraisal came out poorly, there is room for improvement before the next level.

Having completed your appraisals, there are questions you must ask and answer before the next appraisal. These include what was identified that you need to overcome in order for you to move to the next level of life. At individual, personal, marital, or career level; what are the things you must overcome? It could be lateness to work, wasting the whole day on Social Media like Facebook, Instagram, LinkedIn, WhatsApp, or computer games; not getting the kind of results you want, bitterness, anger, hatred, or just being wicked? What must you overcome to qualify for your next level of success? If you think you have nothing to overcome, you have lied to yourself. The Bible says a man's enemies are members of his own household. Your greatest enemies are within, they are not what people do to you, but what you do to yourself, and how you handle your life.

Let me therefore share briefly on the five (5) fundamental steps to achieving greater heights or success in life;

1. **Periodically review yourself**: After you have been reviewed by others, you need to sit back and review yourself. Many people only accept positive reviews, but not the negative ones. You may assume that your supervisor does not like or understand you. Everyone in life has four windows – the open space (what you know that others know about you); hidden (what only you know that nobody else knows about you); blind spot (what others know about you, but you are ignorant of it); and unknown (that part of you that neither you nor anybody knows anything about). This is the Johari Window Model[1]. In leadership, you are encouraged to open up your space so that the blind spot, the hidden spot, and the unknown are minimized, as the more of you people and you know, the better a leader you are. People need to know what you stand for. After review, you must choose to achieve greater heights; you must choose to add another qualification to what you have; and you must choose to add something else to your

---

[1] https://www.communicationtheory.org/the-johari-window-model/

skills and abilities. You need to apply yourself in a unique way. Understand that, you may have done well, yes, but you can do better. If the enemy of your success is attitude or behaviour, then handle them. Life is all about sacrifice. You must go beyond yourself to achieve an objective, that is sacrifice. The Bible says I must work the work of Him while it is still day, for the night cometh when no man shall work. There is time for everything. We must choose to overcome whatever is making us not to succeed. God is not an author of confusion. He says things should be done decently and in order. If it is time to read, you read; time to work, you work; or time to render service, you serve him. That is why we talked about the evil under heaven - spirituality without sensitivity. This has killed many believers. Improve yourself. Add something to what you do. Get better in what you do.

2. **Take deliberate steps**: Nothing good happens by accident. If you want to marry a good wife/husband, take deliberate steps; if you want to get a good job, take deliberate steps; if you want to succeed in life, take deliberate steps; and if you desire to scale new heights, take steps. Only step takers succeed in life.

3. **Plan to succeed**: A wise man said that *failing to plan is planning to fail.* If you are not careful, next year may start and finish with you still where you were 12 months ago if you do not consciously plan to succeed. Plan to succeed in your career and field of work. If you were given a target to reach, plan to exceed it with a good margin.

4. **Empower yourself**: Get the skills, capacity, networks, connections, and tools you need to succeed. Success is not by chance. Empower yourself to succeed. Get what is required, get the mentorship. Bend down, allow yourself to be insulted, but learn from that process. Allow people who you think know more than you to teach you what they know. Don't feel too big to learn. Build up a capacity to carry things that are bigger than you. If you don't have the capacity, you may not scale the new heights. Get empowered.

5. **Depend on God**: No matter how much we try, without God we can do nothing. Work based on Gods guidance because there is a way that *seemeth* right unto a man but the end thereof might be destruction. God facilitates, guides, empowers, sustains and ensures success is achieved.

Get the expertise needed for excellence as you cannot be excellent without the right skillset. The skills for excellence is gotten from continuous innovation. Continuously re-invent yourself as yesterday's excellence maybe today's failure. Continuously improve yourself. Get better in what you do and how you do it by being creative and innovative. You can't afford to waste all your resources.

You cannot be excellent except you are honest and sincere to yourself. When you do well, say "I have done well" and when otherwise, tell yourself "I have not done well but I can do better". Be sincere with those around you because lies, flattery and dishonesty are a burdens you don't want to carry. They hinder your performances and creativity. To succeed therefore, you need to understand that people from different cultural background could be helpers of your destiny so you respect culture and differences. Nobody ever wins Olympic championship without having the passion and zeal to succeed.

In all these things, God should be given his place. If you are occupying a position that you are not qualified for, CHANGE or SHIFT so that somebody who can maximize it can take over that position.

CHAPTER 25

WHY PEOPLE ARE POOR!

Across the world, I have seen various levels of poverty. People were so hungry it could be seen on their faces. Many have not had their salaries for several months. Many find it difficult to pay basic and essential bills, with a number blaming others for their predicaments. This got me thinking. Why are people poor – so poor that they are unable to pay for their primary needs, change their financial levels, and move to a new financial status?

Below are what I think are the common causes of poverty in the present-day world.

1. **Family Traditions:** I am sure you must have heard people who are in desperate situations tell you the stories of their families. They are bold to tell you how difficult life is for them, their forefathers and even their relations and siblings. But many are unwilling to do the things needed to break the family tradition of poverty. It is common to see the children of the rich get richer, but children of the poor get poorer. You may have your theories for this, but I call this

Stagnation at Family Traditions (SFT). The good news is that SFT is not genetic and can be broken. People have over the years destroyed SFT in their lives and families. When a child from a poor home breaks out of this tradition, he/she makes a world of difference. Breaking and destroying SFT is not a chance occurrence. It is a CHOICE occurrence for individuals desiring to scale new heights. You must decide and choose to do what your family has never done before, get out of your comfort zone, fight for your destiny, engage multiple strategies to build multiple streams of income, and be willing to take reasonable and timely risks to escape poverty. It is important for us to remember that doing what our parents did, the way they did them, and living like them are enemies of true change. Remember, *it is madness to do things the same way and expect a different result.* You must reprogram your mind to accept what worked for them, and dissociate yourself from what did not work to create a new destiny and future for yourself.

2. **Missed Opportunities:** People who suffer from Stagnation at Family Tradition (SFT) are regular victims of Missed Opportunities. They see every opportunity as a bait to steal what they have, or a trap of Satan. They think through things so long that they never get to the point of making reasonable decisions. They are experts at analysing every opportunity until they begin to suffer from *Analysis Paralysis (AP).* It is important to understand that people are poor because they either deliberately or otherwise miss good opportunities. Changes,

challenges, and crisis bring opportunities. Only the very bold and sensitive see them. The second world war destroyed and devastated Japan – it also provided an opportunity for the emergence of a superpower economy which is one of the best in the world today. The holocaust destroyed the Jews but led to their infinite exploits in all nations of the world. The Nigerian Civil war killed 2,000,000 Igbos and impoverished the rest through the then Nigerian fiscal policies, but gave the Igbos the impetus to further take over the business world. Recently, there was economic recession in Nigeria. While many were mourning their woes, others saw the opportunities in it and made good money out of the process. Today, government allocations are going down due to crude oil price fluctuation. While some states are not able to pay their workers' salaries, others are declaring surplus. In the programming world, the US system is changing the way they do business. Friends, what opportunities can you see to exploit? Remember, many remain poor because of missed opportunities.

3. **Fear of RISK**: Risk aversion is an enemy of prosperity. Recently, someone asked me for money. I told him I have stopped giving people fish to eat, but have started teaching them how to catch their own fish. Instead of asking me how to begin to catch his own fish, he kept asking me for fish. Why? Risk aversion. People are not willing to put their two feet into the water because of the fear of drowning. Many are afraid to try new things because of the fear of failure. Many are working in systems where they

are not paid for months because of fear of what the world holds for them when they go out there. Many would love to have multiple streams of income, but are afraid to take steps because of fear of losing their capital. Many have seen good opportunities to change their lives but are afraid to take steps because of fear of what may happen. People who are afraid of taking risks usually want to have all the facts before taking steps. This is one major reason people are (or remain) poor. If truly you are afraid of taking steps, why enter a vehicle – it may have accident; why walk on the road – a car may come and kill you; why eat food – it may be poisoned; why breathe in air – it may be contaminated with tuberculosis; why go to work – your boss may not pay you; why buy stuff from the store or markets – they may be bad. Friends, life is all about taking risks. Not taking risk is actually very risky and could be more dangerous than taking the risk. People remain poor because they are risk averse. Improve your risk tolerance and move to the next level.

4. **Laziness and Procrastination:** Excuses, reasons and laziness/procrastination have left many so poor that one can identify them in any crowd. I have over the past few years discovered that laziness and procrastination may run in families. One needs to overcome the traits to make a difference – otherwise poverty will continue to be the identity of the individual. Poor people are lazy in most issues of life. For instance, they are lazy in making decisions, lazy in taking steps, and lazy in continuing at what they began until results are achieved. This

laziness mentality makes them procrastinate over most things – including making decisions, starting something new and continuing a good process.

How to break out of poverty:

To achieve prosperity, the prescription is very simple: First, you must break the family tradition of poverty. Go out of your way to do what your family members have never done – in the positive way. Work hard, but better still, work smart. Secondly, maximize opportunities. Do not just wait for opportunities, search and seek out opportunities and exploit them. See opportunity in every challenge that comes your way, see opportunity in every change – whether positive or negative, see opportunity in every new guideline or policy, see opportunity in everything that happens to you. To maximize these opportunities, thirdly, you must overcome the risk aversion mentality. Rather, be risk tolerant. However, ensure that you analyse the risk and measure its consequences before embarking on any project. Risk tolerance does not imply foolishness or stupidity in the exercising of your capacity to make a difference. Analyse every risk and ensure that you optimize the risk management processes.

Fourthly, take steps. Overcome laziness and procrastination by taking meaningful steps. Get out of your so-called comfort zone. Get out of your bed and go to work. Turn your dreams into projects. Turn your vision into assignment. Turn your wishes into work. Go to work. The antidote of poverty is work. Every successful man is a smart-hard worker.

Your work defines your worth. Do not despise the days of humble beginning, the Bible said. Start somewhere. If you are sensitive, you have all that is required to start – so start. Start your own business, start your own network, start your own shop, join as a volunteer in an organization, and work. And if you cannot work, learn to work.

Finally, to break out of poverty, set some goals for yourself – daily, weekly, monthly and yearly goals. Also set some midterm and long-term goals covering finances, marriage, house, car, career, spirituality, etc. Link your goals to your work and work it out as every achieved goal is somebody's dream turned into work and project. Break out to scale new heights!

CHAPTER 26

CHANGING FINANCIAL LEVELS

After you have handled the challenges posed by *Stagnation at Family traditions, Fear of Taking Risk, Missed Opportunities, and Laziness and Procrastination,* there are some truths you must know. Let us begin with what prophet Isaiah said;

*Arise, shine; for thy light is come, and the glory of the LORD is risen upon thee...*Who are these that fly as a cloud, and as the doves to their windows?... *A little one shall become a thousand, and a small one a strong nation: I the LORD will hasten it in his time.* (Isaiah 60:1, 8& 22)

Whenever light comes, there is a rising and shining. So, if you are not rising or shinning, it means that your light has not come. And when men begin to shine, verse 22 becomes a reality. A little one becomes a great nation, and a small one becomes a strong city. It is important to know that money and wealth are hidden in three main places.

1. ***Money is hidden in People:*** Globally, people are the source of all monies. e.g. doctors call them patients, lawyers call them clients, landlords call them tenants, marketers call them customers, hotels call them guests, employers call them staff or employees, etc. Therefore, the more people you serve, the more money you make. Think of Microsoft, GSM companies, internets, banks, etc. why are they so wealthy? Because they serve many people. *"Show me a man who has made a lot of money, you will see a man who has served millions of people".*

   The more people you serve, the more money you make. If you don't like people, you can't make money. If you hate interacting with people, you can't be wealthy. The money you need for your change in financial level is hidden in people and their pockets.

2. ***Money is hidden in Problems:*** If you normally run away from problems or hate to solve problems, you can never be a wealthy person. Bill Gates is a wealthy man because he had a vision and solved a major world problem. If your desire is to be wealthy, you must be a problem solver, not to abscond from problem. Globally, there are two key problems; ***'Rising poverty and declining health'***. If you are not part of those who want to solve these problems, then you may end up being a problem to yourself. Everybody who is making money out there is solving a problem. Employers pay workers for the problems they solve, problems they avoid

or problems they transform into profits. Therefore, if you want to change financial level, you must see problems as friends and begin to solve them.

3. ***Money is hidden in Opportunities:*** Changes, challenges and crisis offer us great opportunities to make money. We must consciously program ourselves (rather than complaining and murmuring about changes) to maximize opportunities in changes, crisis and challenges. We must look out for what the available opportunities are and explore them.

When our light shines, we arise and "A little one will become a great nation and a small one will be a strong city". We can change financial levels by helping people, solving problems and maximizing opportunities. To do this you must breakout of family traditions. Consciously change the tides of your destiny by taking calculated and reasonable risks. Handle your fears. And more importantly, stop procrastinating on issues. Don't get into a business that makes no sense, that you can't clarify how it flows, grows or if it is sustainable. Get into a business that you can use to change people's life. **P**eople, **O**pportunities and **P**roblems are where money is hidden.

"He will give unto you the hidden treasures of secret places". That means treasures are not in the open. Treasures (wealth) are hidden in people, problems and opportunities. Be people minded, problem focused and an opportunity seeker. THINK PEOPLE, PROBLEM AND OPPORTUNITIES.

You can begin by saving a part of your income monthly – you can save up to 50% of your income if single and 10-20% as a married person. You need to save because when opportunities come, you will need cash. If you are cashless, it won't be possible. Remember, money goes to those that have money. If you have no money in your account and you have opportunities, you may miss them.

My prayer today is that none of us will miss another opportunity in life in Jesus Name.

CHAPTER 27

THE PARABLE OF THE JAMMED DOOR

It was 2300 hours on a Thursday and I decided to check on my nephew who came in from a far city earlier in the day; we had a full house, so he asked to sleep at the boys' quarters. Upon opening the doors and stepping out of the quarters, I was approached by our security officer who narrated an incident that happened in the early hours of the night. It was a case of a "jammed door imprisoning our house help in one of the rooms".

It happened that she was going to attend to a neighbour at dusk, and in attempt to unlock her door, she unknowingly turned the key the wrong way, thereby causing it to break in its place. She got stuck in the room. Although, friends and neighbours made attempts to open the door,they were unable to. Once my security officer was done with the narrative, I made my way back to the room where she was. She was already asleep in the room. I called out her name in an attempt to get her awake while I tried to open the door. I was unable to too. I placed a call for a carpenter to be available early the next morning to get her out of the room. I also requested that my wife and the rest of my family stay back from our early morning church service - Covenant Hour of Prayers - so as to support her release from the room.

Then, the miracle happened. As we began to sing and pray the following day during our morning prayers, she walked in! What a pleasant surprise. She walked in whole and healthy. When asked what happened, she confessed that after I tried and left, she decided to fight for her freedom, and in the process, was able to open the door and free herself. Praise the Lord!

But the question remains, what lessons can we all learn from this? Let me share with you ten fundamental lessons I learnt from it.

1. **Never lock the door of your heart against God, change or divine opportunities.** She did not need to lock the door, but she did. Many people consciously or otherwise lock their lives and destinies out of divine blessings and provisions. Man's greatest enemy is man. Choose not to be an enemy of your life. God is always standing at the doors of our heart knocking. Open and have the best of life. Positive change, and opportunities are always at the doors of our life, do not lock them out. Open, embrace, and enjoy what God has freely provided.

2. **Don't imprison yourself:** Many people imprison themselves knowingly or otherwise. This comes

in the form of addictions, negative choices, and dependencies. Do not imprison yourself. That you never knew it will get so bad is not an excuse. Bad habits can become dangerous addictions that keep you fully imprisoned, as they can make you do things you never wanted to do – steal, lie, cheat, etc. Mind your thoughts as they can become your words, then your actions, character, habits and before you know it, your destiny. Do not imprison yourself with wrong or negative choices in life.

3. **Most pains of life are products of personal mistakes:** She mistakenly locked the door! Our mistakes in life account for most, if not all life's pain. The mistake of going out with the wrong person, taking what does not belong to you, trying out drugs or pornography, testing wrong things, trying to experiment with destiny, marrying the wrong person, going to the wrong school, living in the wrong neighbourhood, worshiping in the wrong church, serving the wrong god, or even having the wrong friends all account for most (if not all) of our life pains. Mistakes make us miss the mark and mark us out for pains and regrets. Mistakes are responsible for life pains. We are free to make any mistake in life, but we may not escape the consequences of the mistakes made.

4. **Every event is an opportunity for new discoveries:** Things happen to us that we cannot explain. However, everything that happens to us is an opportunity to learn, and to discover new things. Our house-help learnt how to open a jammed door. What a major discovery. Please look out for the

learning points in everything that happens to you and your family. Do not close your eyes to the pains of life – otherwise, you will miss the lesson in them. There is always something to learn, and in every life situation, even from failure. Choose to learn.

5. **Never accept the gifts and pains of Satan:** She was imprisoned, and after trying to open the jammed door with the help of friends and neighbours, she gave up, slept off, and was about to accept the negative gifts of Satan until I woke her up, encouraged her by my failed attempt to open the door, and left her motivated. Do not stop trying as your breakthrough is just around the corner. Remember the story of the man that was digging for gold? He stopped just at the 11th hour. You may right now be at your 11th hour. Do not stop. Your morning of joy is around the corner. Keep trying and keep running. Never quit.

6. **God speaks to us in different ways using the simple things of life:** The coming of the neighbours to ask for her help was the opportunity she needed to discover that she had locked herself in. The coming of the deliverer who failed to deliver her was the voice she needed to try again. God speaks to us in a multitude of ways. Stay alive. Stay sensitive. There is a voice always around the corner to set you at liberty. She said that as she continued to try, she noticed things she did not see before, and this gave her solution to her problem. In walking with God, seek out His voice of guidance. You can never work with God and fail. God is speaking right now, are you listening, are you hearing, and will you be willing to obey?

7. **God sends angels to help us in our hour of challenge:** I had no business coming out that late at night – but I did. I had no business using the front door – but I did. This made the security guard see and inform me of the challenge. I came to her as the angel of the moment. The security guard came to me as the angel of the hour. Stop waiting for angels with wings. There are angels of God all around you right now - especially when you are facing a life-threatening situation. God can never leave you alone without a helper of destiny. There are angels working for us, working with us, and working through us. God sends His angels to help us. Receive your angel right now. Her angels came unexpected. Expect yours!

8. **Passion and commitment destroy all impossibilities:** People and friends tried to open the door but failed. She also tried initially, but also failed. But when she said to herself, "maybe there is a blessing awaiting me in tomorrow's prayer hour that Satan is trying to deny me." "What if there is fire now, I cannot escape." Once she had a purpose and complemented this with passion and commitment, the door yielded. Every life challenge is subject to purpose, passion and commitment. It takes you giving yourself a reason to do the right things, to be able to do them.

9. **You need a stimulant to maximize your destiny:** Everyone needs some form of stimulant in life to maximize destiny. We are who we are because of the people we fellowship with, the books we read, and the things we watch. It took my coming out that

night to make her take authority over her life and fight for her life and freedom. Friends, there are destiny refiners and destiny polishers. But there are also destiny blunters and destiny killers. Look out for those that will stimulate you to achieve your life goals.

10. **The real solutions to life challenges are within you:** Many tried to help her, but all failed. Her challenge was triggered by her mistake. Her challenge was resolved by herself. The answer to most life problems are within. Stop looking for external support and helps. You have all it takes to solve most (if not all) life problems. Look inwards. Seek proper introspection. The answer is within you. This means that no man – not father, mother, husband, wife, children or pastors can ever solve your life problem for you. You got to solve them yourself. Please understand this now, and choose to "carry your monkey".

Therefore, never accept no as an answer to satanic suggestion. When others give up, take over and you will surely cross over. When others stop, keep working and keep walking. Your breakthrough is just around the corner. Stopping now will make all previous efforts to be wasted. Keep working at it. Soon, your day of joy will come and you shall arise.

CHAPTER 28

THE REAL MEANING OF SUCCESS

People have defined success as positive achievements in line with set goals. It is also seen as achieving goals, achieving one's desires, achieving your heart desires or what you want or even to excel at something, but, success is not a destination. It is a journey. You never – as long as you are alive – get to a place called success. This is because today's success stories are tomorrow's colossal failures.

Just imagine Peugeot 404. In the 1970s, it was the best car then. If you buy one now, people will think you are mad. Think also of the house your father built in the '70/80s? Then it was a masterpiece, but today, if not reworked, it becomes an eyesore. Where are yesterday's successful individuals? Where are the best students in your class in those days? Where are the sports champions in your youthful days? Many are no longer remembered. Why? Once successful does not mean always successful.

Success is not a destination. Work to succeed, one step at a time. Work to enjoy not just the "dreamed" destination, but, more importantly, the journey. I have heard people say, "When I get married, I will be happy." What an illusion. Once you find the person, the challenges of getting married will face you daily. Once you marry, the challenges of living with the individual comes. Once you marry the person of your dreams, the problems of pregnancy, childbirth, child upbringing, etc. emerge. Issues and challenges never end. Do not postpone your happiness waiting for the day of success, enjoy the journey.

Learn to celebrate every win and enjoy every day (no matter how small). What do we need to have continued success every day every time? Follow these five simple steps and life will be better for you and all.

1. **Have a dream or a vision that is bigger than you.** Success begins with a change in mind-set. As you change your mind, you can change your life and your world.
2. **Develop a plan to achieve your dream or vision.** Recall that failure to plan, is planning to fail. Plan, and revise until you have a good and workable plan.
3. **Work your plan – one step at a time.** Success is linked to action, and successful people are always on the move. Take a step today. Stop procrastinating. Make moves. Until you move, nothing moves.
4. **Review your progress at every defined point in your journey.** This could be every week, month, year or at particular defined milestones.

5. **Make corrections where you derail and celebrate your little successes.** Remember Deming's Plan: Do, Study and Act cycle. Keep improving and soon, you will be the greatest.

Remember, success does not come to you, you go to it. Begin or continue the journey towards success now. You will succeed. I will share the five S of success in the next Chapter

CHAPTER 29

THE 5S OF SUCCESS

Luke 2 verse 43, 47 and 48;

⁴³And when they had fulfilled the days, as they returned, the child Jesus tarried behind in Jerusalem; and Joseph and his mother knew not of it....⁴⁶And it came to pass, that after three days they found him in the temple, sitting in the midst of the doctors, both hearing them, and asking them questions. ⁴⁷And all that heard him were astonished at his understanding and answers. ⁴⁸And when they saw him, they were amazed....

The child Jesus tarried behind and because he tarried to learn, listen and ask questions from better and greater minds; he became an amazement not only to the people who heard him speak, but also to his parents and relations. To bring out the best in you, to maximize your potentials, to become a person of excellence, and impact; you must do the extra, go the extra mile and pay the required price. For instance, in life, I have come to discover that being a person of 8 – 5 (i.e. 8.00 am to 5.00 pm) working hours can never make you a success. Working for only 8 hours in a 24 hours day will never make you wealthy; 8 – 5, Mondays – Fridays can never make you sufficient, prosperous or fulfilled! Let me put it this way, 8 – 5 will make you a servant for life and I mean, for life. There is no great man anywhere whose wealth was made between 8 – 5, not even thieves and corrupt leaders!

Why? Because between 8 – 5, you're doing other people's work, you're participating in meetings you didn't schedule, you're responding to people's issues and phone calls, you're solving other people's problems, and you hardly ever have any time to work on your own agenda for the day. It is deciding to stay back after 5.00pm, put in some extra time that distinguishes you from the rest. The extra effort put in after official work-hours when the environment is calm and quiet that brings out the best in you, and sets you apart for excellence and success. If therefore you desire the Jesus kind of amazement in life, then you must learn to tarry (even when it hurts!).

Most people actually do not even work for 8 – 5 and still they want miracles. Some arrive work late and leave early. Some pack up their bags and materials 30 minutes before closing time and spend the rest of the day chatting or indulging in unprofitable ventures. Still they want the best of testimonies and successes – friends, it does not happen that way. Take out time and speak to any successful student who had a first class or successful business man who has risen from the floor, and you will discover that one of their major secrets is working extra time, tarrying on their books or work when all others have left, or just doing the extra to get the extra points. If we do not, therefore, put in an extra effort, go the extra mile, either in our work, family, career, spiritual life etc., we can't be great.

Friends you cannot be great working 8 -5. This is my candid advice. Make sure you're not an 8 -5 person. Greatness starts from 5.00 pm. You must choose to invest your 5 – 8 hours. If you want to be like Jesus, you must be an 8am–8am person, you must go beyond the status quo, you must put in extra effort, you must be more than ready to go the extra mile. To achieve our dreams and aspirations in life, we must be willing to go the extra miles, make the extra efforts and invest our 5 to 8 hours, then greatness will be ours.

In life, you're not a failure until you accept failure. Everyone has failed at some points in their lives. Show me a man/woman who has never failed, and you have seen a man/woman who never did anything. Friends, it is better to fail and rise than never to do anything at all. But you can reduce your struggles and pains towards success by simple steps. These are what I have called the **5S** to success. Anyone can succeed. Everyone should succeed. But success is not free. There is a price to pay for the prize of success. Do you want to succeed, then take note of these 5S of success;

1. **Sensitivity**: Be sensitive to the time and seasons of your life. Be sensitive to the times we are in. Be sensitive to your environment within and around your office, home and even play field. There are so many benefits you can gain by just being sensitive.

Be sensitive to the things you hear from the mouth of your mentors, see in others and participate in. It could change your life forever.

2. **Spirituality**: Be spiritual. Your sensitivity is heightened by your spirituality. The more of God you know, the better life becomes for you. Everyone says they have decided to hand things over to God, but friends you may be handing over to God what he has already handed over to you, and so you end up frustrated. If you don't hear from God, if you can't see God, and if you can't understand Him, then you will be saying, "I'm waiting on God", when actually, you are just wasting your life. Be spiritual. Make sure that at every point in time you are sensitive and you are spiritual. These are the hallmarks of success.

3. **Sacrifices**: Make sacrifices. Everyone that succeeds in life makes sacrifices. Show me a man/woman who has succeeded, and I will show you a person of sacrifice! It may or may not be financial. Sacrifices could be with time, pleasure, resources, etc. Success requires an element of sacrifice. The greater the sacrifice, the greater the degree and rate of success.

4. **Servant-hood mentality**: Have a servant-hood mentality. Learn to be humble. Until you learn to learn from others, you may never amount to anything. If you don't learn how to be a good follower, you can never be an effective leader. Have a servant-hood mentality. Understand that we are here to serve. If someone is younger than you but has what you need, please respect him/her and stoop to learn

from the person. You never know what would drop from him/her that could change your life forever positively.

5. **Service**: Our values are determined by the services we render. Your reward is a function of the service you provide. If you are not providing any service, then you have no reward. Learn to serve, learn to be useful both to yourself and your environment. Learn to add values through service to man and to God. Never waste another minute of your life waiting on who should and would serve you. Service turns a servant into a success.

These are the 5S that deliver success. When you are sensitive; spiritual; you make the right sacrifice; have a servanthood mentality; and you are willing to serve others, your community, and your environment, then you are qualified to succeed.

If you refuse any or all of these 5S, then you will struggle, sweat, suffer, be stagnated and enjoy sorrow resulting in shame.

You have a choice to make. You either choose the 5S of success or the 5S resulting from failure – sweating, suffering, stagnation, sorrow and shame. Make the right choices that will move you forward forever.

PART 3

STRATEGIES

CHAPTER 30

THE SECRET OF GREATNESS

Every success in life is premised on a trade secret, and every great man has a unique secret. The reason Coca-Cola and Pepsi are not the same is because of their trade secrets; the reason *Peak Milk, Nano* or *Cowbell* are not the same is because of their secrets. They all use milk from cows as raw materials, but after processing, the results are different. To become great, there are things great people do which they may never reveal to others. The difference between a nonentity and an achiever is the secret they operate by. What is the secret of greatness?

Proverbs 18:1*Through desire a man, having separated himself, seeketh and intermeddleth with all wisdom.*

The primary secret of greatness is the **desire for greatness**. You can be big without thinking great, but you can't be great without thinking big! It takes desire to move away from where you are to where you ought to be. As long as you don't have the desire for greatness, greatness will only remain an illusion to you. For instance, why do I work long hours and sometimes into the night? My desire for greatness.

President Muhammadu Buhari is the Nigerian president from 2015 till when I was writing this book. Even though he may not have all the skills for the work, he was voted in because of his persistent desire to become the president. Similarly, Donald Trump became the President of the United States of America through desire. People may say that they lack the right skills and qualifications for a president, but they still got there through desire.

Greatness begins from your desire, but it does not end with desire. The Bible says, *through desire a man having separated himself....* True desire galvanizes actions towards the achievement of the desire.

...Through desire a man, having separated himself... Desires makes you seek out a quiet place to meditate, work on and develop yourself.

In Genesis 24:63, Isaac went on a retreat and returned with his wife. In Genesis 32:24, Jacob was left alone and he ended up with a changed name and his new destiny was revealed to him by the angel. Moses went to the mountain top in Exodus 3:1, and returned a leader following his encounter with the burning bush. Jesus took time off in Luke 4:1&14 to go and fast alone, and upon His return, His fame spread abroad. Paul was called into the Ministry by Jesus Christ himself, he consulted with no man, nor ran to Jerusalem, but rather went to Arabia for three years for a personal retreat (Galatians 1:17). Upon his return, he turned the world upside down.

It is not the length of the retreat that matters, but the desire to have one, and the willingness to maximize it. Isaac's retreat was just for a few hours, Jesus was for 40 days and 40 nights, but Paul's was for three years. Well utilized retreats result in the birth of new destinies!

There are five types of people who normally go for retreats. First set are those who go because it's their organization's policy. Second set are those that go because of the short-term benefits attached to the retreat such as free meals, allowances and accommodation in the best hotels that they can't normally afford. Third set are those who see it as an opportunity to relax and/or an avenue to run away from family challenges. The fourth set are those who want to update their curriculum vitae. The last set are those who go because of their need to move forward in life and scale new heights.

Through desire, a man having separated himself... so, Isaac found a wife, Jacob found a destiny, Moses found a mission, Jesus found fame, Paul found a life – all in retreats.

It is therefore important to understand that greatness begins with a desire. Once desire is present, you should step back, reflect, meditate and think through things. The very best time to re-access your self is after your last testimony. You should not allow your previous victory derail your destiny and give you the arrival mentality. Yesterday's victory is tomorrow's failure if not improved upon. After your last testimony, you will find out that you have more mountains to conquer.

Greatness starts with the desire for greatness, and the steps to greatness include reflection, retreat and meditation.

CHAPTER 31

POSITIONING FOR GREATNESS

It is important to understand that greatness is real, greatness is achievable, greatness is realizable; but greatness is not cheap. Many may desire to be great, but very few people are usually willing to pay the prize for greatness. Understand that God has made us agents of change, people that can change the world. However, we cannot change the world except we are great enough to change the world. To be able to be great in life, there is a position we must take that makes all the difference. What is this position?

Number 27:16 & 18

16 Let the Lord, the God of the spirits of all flesh, set a man over the congregation,....18 And the Lord said unto Moses, Take thee Joshua the son of Nun, a man in whom is the spirit, and lay thine hand upon him;

The question is why was Joshua, who was not in the lineage of Moses, lineage of Aaron nor lineage of Mariam, selected? Moses had children, he had sons and daughters, Moses had a brother (Aaron) who also must have had sons and daughters, Moses had a sister who may have had her own sons and daughters. But none from Moses' lineage was selected to succeed him. Why was Joshua chosen for this next level of leadership? The answer is very simple. Joshua positioned himself for greatness!

Several times in the scriptures in the book of Exodus, Numbers, and Leviticus, Joshua was seen following Moses on many divine assignments, whether he was invited or not. Forty days, Moses was before God at the mountain top hearing from and fellowshipping with God. What we hardly ever recognize is that Joshua also was at the base of the mountain waiting on his master. Joshua, by self-selection, chose to fast, wait and be part of his master's assignments. He left his family and friends to follow Moses. So, when it was time for Moses to depart and he had to appoint somebody to take over from him, God did not choose Moses' first, or second son, or third son, nor any from his lineage. Although, they may have the physical qualifications, but Joshua, the son of Nun, a man in whom is the spirit was chosen as the replacement. So, Moses was asked to lay his hand on Joshua so as to transfer some of the honor in him to the new ruler/Judge.

Similarly, in the world today, we see a lot of surprises. Individuals who are not related to the current leaders may take over some positions. Position, therefore, yourself for greatness. The selection of most people for some specific assignments is a product of several years of positioning and repositioning. What is then the qualification that empowered Joshua to access the greatness and honor that was in Moses?

1. **Humility**: Be humble. Be meek. Be willing to stand and accept all manner of corrections and chastisement from people. Be willing to learn from those who have gone ahead of you. Joshua understudied Moses, and at the right time, he was appointed to take over from Moses. He paid the prizes of servant-hood. I say commonly that you cannot enjoy the prize until you pay the price. Be willing to pay the price. Until you follow, you can't lead. It's only true followers that end up becoming great leaders.

Many want to lead without the preparation. It doesn't work that way! Leadership begins from followership. You must follow effectively to lead effectively. When you think you know it all, then you lack the skills and everything that is needed to lead. Joshua followed until he became the best, and from nowhere he was appointed to take over from Moses. After Joshua, nobody took-over from him because nobody paid the price Joshua paid. Even his own children couldn't take over from him and thus were lost completely from the system. All the young men and women around him were lost completely too. This led to several years when there was leadership vacuum, until when the judges came. The vacuum shows that, irrespective of the need, God will not give you what you are not qualified for. God will also prefer to have a vacuum than to position you in a place you are not qualified for. That is why what we have in Leviticus 21 is so important.

There is one thing you must do away with if you must be an effective follower.

2. **Blemish:**

Leviticus 21:18

*¹⁸**For whatsoever man he be that hath a blemish, he shall not approach...***

Positioning for greatness requires that you do away with all blemishes and there are three categories of blemish. These include, physical blemish, emotional blemish and spiritual blemish. As a leader in the making, you must do away with

1. Physical blemish which could be nature induced (like crippling, deafness, dumbness, etc.) or *self-induced physical blemish* such as mouth and body odors, irresponsible dressing, etc. Physical blemishes affect your leadership efficiency.
2. Emotional blemish such as bitterness, envy, anger, hatred, and wickedness as they block the mind from thinking rationally, and a life from making sustainable progress. Many are burdened with emotional blemish against themselves, their neighbors, relatives, co-workers, etc. These stop them from accessing greatness in life. It is time to apply your mind to productive thinking – for as a man thinketh in his heart, so is he.
3. Spiritual blemish denies you access to heaven's grace and helps. Man may benefit from human helps and connections, but divine helps and connection

are what make you achieve greatness in life. Spiritual blemish denies you from having the right connection with God and this cuts short your greatness journey. When you are connected to God, He makes your life meaningful.

Learn therefore to position yourself for greatness. Choose to go forward and to be the best you can be in life. Everything about life is based on choice. By our own personal choices and positioning (or repositioning), God shall make us great. Therefore, position yourselves for greatness.

CHAPTER 32

THE DANGERS OF ASSUMPTIONS

It's very easy for us to assume that things will happen the way they happened before. But, in the race of life, things do not always happen in the usual (or expected way). When I wrote this chapter, Donald Trump just won the US Presidential election. Many of us assumed that he was a joker, that he had no chance and just came to have fun. With seasoned politicians in both republican and democratic parties, we were sure that he had no chance. But he won. And he has been in government for over a year now. I listened briefly to his acceptance speech. What an upset!

All our assumptions – he had never held a government position, he was never in the armed forces, his speeches were hurtful and all that – which we thought would work against him had actually worked for him. Assumptions may be dangerous and destructive. That you came to work and there were no traffic challenges do not mean it will be the same tomorrow. That you spend $2,000 for the whole month and was able to meet all your needs, does not mean you will spend the same amount in the next month. That you missed work and no one noticed, does not mean you will still go unnoticed if it happens again. I am not saying that assumptions are always wrong, as you cannot live your life without assumption. But be careful before making them!

A lesson from Joshua will further elaborate this.

Joshua 7:2–3: *² And Joshua sent men from Jericho to Ai, which is beside Bethaven, on the east of Bethel, and spake unto them, saying, "Go up and view the country". And the men went up and viewed Ai.³ And they returned to Joshua, and said unto him, "**Let not all the people go up; but let about two or three thousand men go up and smite Ai; and make not all the people to labour thither; for they are but few".***

They had a good reason to believe that they did not need a whole army to win Ai. By the way, they just demolished Jericho a few days/months earlier (Joshua 6:20). They were sure of their capacity to win wars. Thus, their assumption that Ai was too small to need their entire army. But how wrong they were…

Joshua 7:4–5: *⁴ So there went up thither of the people about three thousand men: and they fled before the men of Ai. ⁵ And the men of Ai smote of them about thirty and six men: for they chased them from before the gate even unto Shebarim, and smote them in the going down: wherefore the hearts of the people melted, and became as water.*

*... Let not all the people go up...*They were so sure of themselves. How wrong they were! The victories of yesterdays usually make us so sure, so proud of ourselves. This is usually a very dangerous assumption.

When God came in, He asked them to go with all the men of war in Chapter 7 verse 1. What a great mistake. Their wrong assumption led to their disgrace, their defeat and the death of 36 men. You will not be defeated. Please understand that things we neglect could lead to our destruction. A little drop of kerosene is enough to destroy the entire pot of soup. What we consider to be insignificant may turn out to be most significant. Am I telling you not to assume? No, but here are the three important things on which assumptions must be based:

1. **Correct and Current Facts**: Assumptions must be based on correct and current facts, and not merely on past victories. This is because, circumstances can and do change. Our assumptions must be based on current events, current happenings and current analysis, and not just on what you think. We must realize that facts change on daily basis, facts change every time. When we begin to look back to what we have achieved in our lives, in our profession and in our family, we tend to take a lot of things for granted. Please understand, that you got things right the first time, does not mean subsequently things will go right. This is where sensitivity comes in place.

2. **Sensitivity**: Assumptions must be based on high level of sensitivity. You must be sensible and

sensitive to the times and seasons of life so as not to suffer the traumas of life. It will be so foolish to think that things will continue to occur in the same way. The Israelites destroyed Jericho, not with the energy of the flesh, but with God on their side and through obedience to divine instructions. But with Ai, they went on their own – without seeking God's involvement. Be sensitive. Not every victory is self-induced. Recognize all the helpers of your destiny. That is why, you must develop strategic alternatives.

3. **Strategic Alternative:** Always ask yourself, "What if this does not work?" "What if something goes wrong?" "What if I am wrong?" Answers to these questions will help you develop strategic alternatives before the need arises. Have an alternative plan, and make alternative arrangements.

People have wasted their lives based on some wrong assumptions they made. Many women have fallen into the trap of the wicked men as a result of foolish assumptions. Recently, a British in South Korea was sentenced to life imprisonment because he killed two young girls in cold blood. He promised them a lot of money, but they ended up dying following severe tortures and abuses. Before you take that step, be careful. That is why you must have a defined vision in life to scale new heights.

CHAPTER 33

THE POWER OF VISION

One wise woman, Helen Keller, said and I paraphrase "the worst tragedy in life is not the absence of sight, but the absence of vision." Helen Keller became deaf and blind at the age of 19 months, but she attained the throne of grace and glory, doing exploits all through her lifetime. She wrote books, went to school, and was a political activist. When people who have gone ahead of you speak, please listen. She said that the worst tragedy in life is not the absence of sight (physical), but absence of vision.

Vision defines destinies, visions make everyday of your life meaningful. Vision takes away the burden of living and gives you the enjoyment of success. It takes vision to wake up early in the morning and jump out of your bed knowing you have something to do that day. It takes vision not to have high blood pressure on a Monday morning because you are going to work. It takes vision to live your life and leave a legacy at the end of the day. That you have eyesight is not an achievement, but you having a vision, is a great achievement. This is because, unlike eyesight, your vision is self-determined. Every day of your life that you live without a vision is a wasted day as you will end up not achieving as much as you should have achieved. Vision is the fuel of success.

Proverbs 29:18

Where there is no vision, the people perish: but he that keepeth the law, happy is he.

Time is always on the move. Have you been able to define your current year's vision? What is that thing that you must achieve before the end of this year? What is that thing that must happen this year - not by chance but by choice? Certain good things happen to us by chance, but most good things happen by choice. What should happen this year that by December 31st you would say, "Yes God, this year you have helped me to achieve this"?

Vision is not all about making money or building houses. These are all great visions, but friends, you must have a true vision that goes beyond that and drives you to be/do something greater. Vision is not external, it is internal, so if you have none, it's a choice. Visions are multi-faceted, you can have visions in different areas of your life: spiritual, financial, academic, marital, intellectual etc. The truth is, if you do not have a vision to run with this year, you will arrive at 31st December wondering what happened. And you know the truth, nothing would have happened.

If you say, "before the end of this year, I would be married", that is a vision and you should work towards it. Or, "before December this year, I would have finished my degree program." You should work towards it. My advice is that you identify a project or program in life that drives you and motivates you to do well in life.

Vision makes all the difference, for where there is no vision, the people perish. Let us look at that passage from other versions;

Proverbs 29:18 (NIV)

Where there is no revelation, people cast off restraint; but blessed is the one who heeds wisdom's instruction.

Proverbs 29:18 (Message)

If people can't see what God is doing, they stumble all over themselves; but when they attend to what he reveals, they are most blessed.

When there is no revelation, people cast off restraints, so they just take whatever happens to them. They stumble over themselves. You know why people fight for things that do not make sense? It is because they cannot see who they are or where they are going. They all walk in darkness and stumble. And when you keep stumbling, good progress is hindered. Friends, many are stumbling every day.

Do you know why people are jealous of one another? Why they are envious? They have no vision. People stumble because they lack vision. Please understand that not having a vision is not God's fault or your father's fault, but it is your fault.

Having a vision is one thing, successfully managing your vision to its accomplishment is another. Diligence is the primary requirement for a successful vision management.

Proverbs 22:29

Seest thou a man diligent in his business? He shall stand before kings; he shall not stand before mean men.

Diligence refers, not to hard work alone, but rather to SMART WORK.

Hard work + Intelligence = Smart work; Hard work – Intelligence = *Sweat-fullness*.

Do not just have a vision for a better tomorrow and walk around telling everybody you meet; rather work it out through smart works. "I want to build a house this year", work towards it; "I want to buy a car this year", work towards it; "I want to make a difference in my village this year", work towards it. Do not just stumble all through your destiny this year, work towards it! Whatever you have purposed to do, work towards it. Friends, diligence is the primary requirement for a successful vision. Anybody can have great ideas, but where there is no diligence, they are just wishes. A wise man said "if wishes were horses, beggars would ride."

Some may even have well documented visions in their books describing what they would achieve, but they don't have a "how" to achieve it. What to achieve is good, but how to achieve it is also very important. Once you have what you want to achieve, then begin to work on how to get there. The "how" of a thing is what we call **strategy**. It is the strategy that makes all the difference.

If you do not have a vision, begin to work on it. Wake up every morning and begin to fine tune your vision. One thing is to have a vision, and another is to have a strategy on how to achieve it. Turn your vision into a dream.

CHAPTER 34

DARE TO DREAM - AGAIN!

Many of us have aspirations in life of the things we would love to accomplish, but are afraid to take a step towards achieving them. We look at others and desire to have what they have, but hardly work to find out what they do or are doing to have them. I ask you to dare to dream. And peradventure you have dreamed before, and it did not come to pass, dare to dream again!

Dreams are the raw materials of greatness. Joseph had a dream. He dreamt more than once. In his dreams, he saw his brothers and parents bowing to him. He later became a dream interpreter, and this brought him before Pharaoh and later made him a Prime Minister. Pharaoh's baker and his cupbearer dreamt, and their dreams came to pass. Several kings and leaders in the scripture like Pharaoh, Nebuchadnezzar, Daniel etc. all had dreams. It is critical that at every point in time of your life, you are dreaming of something. Not just something, but something great. Most of life's inventions were peoples' dreams. Today, the big houses, vehicles, airplanes, etc. that we see, and use were formally people's dreams.

It is important to have your own dreams. These will help you to set goals and priorities for your life. Dreams are powerful. Friends, if you can dream it, then you can become it. Turn your big vision into a big dream!

Psalm 37:4

⁴ Delight thyself also in the LORD: and he shall give thee the desires of thine heart.

It is important to know that God is in support of dreams, as long as it is line with His will and as we delight always in Him, he will guide us into fulfilling them.

What are the basic steps you must take to both dare to dream and see your dream come to pass?

1. **Eliminate Self-doubt and low self-esteem**: A man's enemies are members of his own household – the Bible says. Let us say it another way – A man's enemies are primarily within. Until you overcome them, you may never achieve without! For instance, a number of self-destructive thoughts may be going through your mind - "Who am I to think this big?" "How will I possibly achieve this?" These may run through our minds when we begin to think of some great things. Self-doubt and low self-esteem do hinder dreams. Before anyone can believe in you, you must first believe in yourself.

Low self-esteem is an enemy of big dreams. Understand that, no matter what you are thinking about, you can achieve it. A wise man said, "if you can think about it, then it is possible". It all depends on your mindset and how you make yourself available to God. Therefore, to achieve great dreams, eliminate self-doubt and low self-esteem.

2. **Face your FEARs**. The fear factor hinders us from daring to dream (or dream again). The bigger the dream, the more likely there would be FEAR. Zig Ziglar said "Fear has two meanings; *Face Everything and Rise or Forget Everything and Run*, the choice is yours". The ball is in your courts. You can choose to apply whatever meaning of fear that suits you to your dreams. In order to dream big, you have to block out your past, face the current circumstance, and rise to your glorious future. If the fulfilment of your dream is what you want, you must face everything and rise. Remember, that fear also means false evidences appearing real. It is important to realize that most of the things you fear NEVER come to pass. Rise up and face it. You can overcome, and with God, you will overcome.

3. **Maximize every opportunity**: Life is a function of the opportunities you explore, not the chances you missed. All dreams are linked to opportunities and dreams can only come to pass when the dreamer is able to identify opportunities linked to the dream and maximize them. Act on opportunities! Opportunities are all around us, but most of us are not ready to use them. Most often than none, opportunities come indirectly; sometimes as work – you having to

do something you do not enjoy or maybe stepping out of your comfort zone to explore new things. It takes wisdom to identify an opportunity. This is the reason we have to always be in tune with God, as He still divinely guides people to identify and grab opportunities that will advance their destinies. Look out for good opportunities, and choose today to act on opportunities as they come.

4. **Walk with God**: The text scripture says; *"Delight thyself also in the LORD: and he shall give thee the desires of thine heart"*. Without God, we can do nothing. It takes the hand of God on our lives to have our desires come to pass. Every good gift comes from God. If your dreams are good, you need God in it; if they are powerful and wonderful, you need God in it. It is, therefore, important that you delight yourself in God; take pleasure in the things He takes pleasure in and He'd give you the desires of your heart. If you apply yourself to what God wants you to do, He'd help you supernaturally attain your heart desires.

For instance, God places in our hearts desires that may point us to our potentials. These are seeds of greatness. Depending on how you nurture the seed inside of you, it can grow to become a mighty tree which many will come and take shade under or it can die without seeing the light of the day. We encourage you to use these seeds to maximize your potential. Therefore, make it a daily habit to seek guidance from the Lord. Grow in the word, listen to Him, maintain a quiet spirit, live a life of humility and open yourself to the voice of God.

5. **Run with Patience**: We live in a fast paced world; fast food, fast money, fast results, fast airplanes, fast internet, fast car, etc. The Bible enjoins us to "follow them, who through patience obtained the promise" (Hebrews 6:12). Most times when we believe God for something and it doesn't come to pass as we desired it, we lose faith immediately, become angry with God and most times change focus. Beloved, let us understand that some things just take time. *You can't* produce a *baby* in *one month* by *getting nine women pregnant* (Warren Buffet). Joseph's dream took over 17 years to come to pass. When you have done all, wait!!! And while waiting, water your seed and talent.

Please understand that if your dreams can be achieved by you, then you do not need God. To need God, your dreams must be bigger than you. Dare to dream – or dream again! Do not let your potentials die within you. Our prayer for you this year is that you will dream bigger dreams that will come through in Jesus Christ's name.

CHAPTER 35

HOW BIG IS YOUR VISION AND DREAMS?

Recently, I read a statement of a young man I admire – King Solomon of the Bible. The Bible recorded that he determined to build a house for God. In his words, the house which he was about to build was to be "wonderful great" (2Chronicles 2:9). Look at the description –wonderful great!

How big or great is your vision? He determined to do what was wonderful and great. What have you chosen to use your life to do? Small things? Irrelevant things? Mediocre things? Or great things? Remember, as a man thinks in his heart so is he.

If your mind cannot conceive it, your hands will never handle it. Stop limiting yourself. You can do wonderful and great things. You have both the capacity and time – go for it!

Wonderful and great things are not products of birth, qualifications, connections or even beauty and size; they are products of the right mindset, right dreams and visions, and right motivation. Many are living as chickens when they should be eagles. Many are dying as dogs when they were created to be lions. Many are walking on the ground, when they should be flying in the air. How big is your dream and vision?

A man without dreams and vision is a disaster about to happen. If in life, you are just living to work, pay your bills, marry, have children and die; you are of all men/women most miserable. What shall you be remembered for? The food you ate? The wife/husband you married? The children you delivered? Or the impacts you made?

Stop surviving. Stop existing. Start living. Work to live and leave a worthy legacy. True living is leaving a legacy for all to see and enjoy. Like Steve Jobs, work to put a dent on the globe. Like Solomon, leave a story for others to read. Like Obama, have a mind for great things. Like Luther, work to change the status quo. Like Mandela, fight injustice. Like Nike, get over your shortcomings and disabilities. Like Jordan, be the best you could be.

Remember, you can make a difference. I ask you to work to leave a legacy. Build a destiny around a great dream and vision. Start today. Start now by thinking self employment – entrepreneurship. There are two kinds of people on earth – those employed by others; and those that employ them. Which do you like or want to be?

CHAPTER 36

MAXIMIZING MENTORSHIP

Isaac Newton said, "If I have seen further than others, it is by standing upon the shoulders of giants." On whose shoulder are you standing?

Everyone and anyone needs a mentor. And when I say a mentor, I am not limiting it to a mentor in your academic or work career, but mentors in every area of life - profession, marriage, financial life, ministry and even fatherhood or motherhood. Are you a newly married couple? You can look out for those who have gone ahead of you, who have done well in their marital life, and choose them as your mentors. As a fresh graduate aiming at becoming an expert in your field of expertise, try and identify someone who has gone ahead of you and learn from them. Standing on the shoulder of giants shortens your learning curve, minimizes mistakes and facilitates higher and greater achievements.

Hear what one of the greatest kings that ever lived on earth – David – has to say, "They looked unto him, and were lightened: and their faces were not ashamed." (Psalm 34: 5). Paul, one of the greatest apostles that ever lived had this to say, "Be ye followers of me; even as I also am of Christ" (1 Corinthians 11:1)

Mentorship has three main benefits to the mentee:

1. It lightens the burden of challenges, mistakes and obstacles. It minimizes toiling, frustrations and depressions. When you have a good mentor, he/she helps you carry your life, career, marital, ministry or financial burdens; and by so doing making the burden lighter for you to carry. Marriage mentors minimize marriage challenges and quarrels, financial mentors prevent debts and poverty, ministry mentor prevents crisis and failure, professional mentors open new doors for you in your career. We need mentors that will lighten our burdens.
2. They enlighten your mind. Mentors bring about better understanding of issues of life, finances, ministry, career, profession and even health. There are so much you may never see or know, until somebody shows you or tells you. Having the right mentor opens you up to new things and new ways of doing things. Yes! Mentors guide you to succeed with minimal stress and challenges. An adage puts it this way, "what an old man sees while sitting, a young man jumping can never see it." Friends, you need the wisdom of the aged (i.e. mentors) to make the needed differences in life.
3. It destroys shames. Life is daily challenged with shame facilitating issues. Mentorship removes

past shames and prevents future shame. It takes a mentor to guide you away from all forms of shame. Asking the right questions from the right people prevents failures and errors – erasing shame!

With mentors, you understand things better, have access to higher levels of knowledge, and struggle less to achieve greater result. Progression in life becomes easier when you are linked to a mentor. So, mentorship is critical to a life of success. There are burdens you are carrying now that can be offloaded if you have a good mentor around you. There are levels of ignorance that you can destroy by just having the right people around you. It is, therefore, self-destructive to say, "I am a man of myself"; "I do not need anybody in my life"; "I can do it by myself"; or "I can achieve it by myself". I do not doubt your capacity to get the work done, but doing it all by yourself will take you a longer time as well as cost you more. For instance, it's better to be a millionaire at 30 than at 80. What will you use the money for? It's better to build your palace at 40 than building it at 100 when you may not have the strength to climb the staircase. It's better to buy the best brand of car at 30 and enjoy it than to buy it at 100 when you can't even drive. Yes, you can be a man of yourself, but it will take you a longer time to achieve your goals than linking up with those who have gone ahead of you and learning from them.

Maximize mentorship! Who is your mentor? Professionally, who is your mentor? In your marital life, who is your mentor? Spiritually, who is your mentor? Financially, who is your mentor? You can have different mentors at different times and for different areas of life. However, there are enemies of mentorship. Below are the common fundamental enemies of mentorship?

1. **Pride:** People are too proud to submit themselves, and too proud of who they think they are. Anybody can learn from anybody. The wisest man who ever lived, Solomon learned from everything – the ant (Proverbs 6:6), spider, lion, locust, cronies, goat, etc. (Proverbs 30:25-31). He learned from a lazy man (Proverbs 12:27). In short, Solomon learned from everything. He says, *"And I gave my heart to seek and search out by wisdom concerning all things that are done under heaven: this sore travail hath God given to the sons of man to be exercised therewith."* (Ecclesiastes 1:13). Thinking you don't need to learn from anybody will make you rigid and un-improving. Get a mentor. Get somebody that can help you to get to the next level of life. You have struggled enough on your own, it's time to climb upon the shoulders of others and ride on it. The second enemy of mentorship is…

2. **Ignorance:** When I say ignorance, I mean unconsciously unconscious ignorance. That is, you know nothing, and you do not even know that you know nothing – and maybe deceiving yourself thinking that you know something. Some people have a kind of mentality that makes them think that they know it all. Stop deceiving yourself – that is the worst form of self-deceit! Open up your eyes to see how ignorant you are…. The third enemy of mentorship…

3. **Blindness:** Beyond mental blindness (ignorance), there are those who are also physically blind. They are blinded to people God or destiny has placed on their way of success as mentors. They cannot recognize their helpers of destiny. I am a full beneficiary of helpers of destiny. I could never have gotten to where I am today without them. Sometimes, because they are physically blind, they may even work against their helpers of destiny.

   The truth is that everybody needs helps, even the mighty. Here David said again, *"...I have laid help upon one that is mighty;..."* (Psalm 89:19). You need help. Open up your eyes to see your God ordained helpers of destiny and maximize them. The fourth and last enemy of mentorship I shall be discussing is

4. **Curses of life:** Curses are real, and many are victims of curses. Curses may come from God, man, family, witches, or even self. There are some of us who are operating under the influence of curses from their villages. Sometimes, when you are about to breakthrough, something bumps in and derails your life. Curses of life are real and they make life difficult. You have to ensure that such curses are broken and your destiny liberated from its effects and impacts.

   Everyone needs a mentor; somebody s/he can look up to; and learn from. God will open your eyes to see your mentor(s) and helpers of destiny; and grant you boldness/meekness to link up with them to grow as you ride on their shoulders to highest heights in life.

CHAPTER 37

EXCELLENT GUIDE FOR OUTSTANDING RESULTS IN LIFE

1. **Set a target.** Excellence begins with a target. What do you want to achieve in life this week, month or year? Where do you want to be by the end of the year? I do not mean a ceremonial target that only less than 3% honor, but targets backed by strategies to achieve them. Remember, playing a football match without a goal post is similar to playing for fun! Have a defined destination for your life, and document it. You should have different targets – for your career, academics, finances, family, social life, spirituality, and community development. Always work with God to set the right targets for the year.

2. **Strategize to achieve your target.** Targets without strategies are foundations for failure and frustrations. A wise man said, (I completely agree with him),"failure to plan is planning to fail". The fact is that your inability to develop strategies equals your decision not to succeed.

Things always happen to targets – and they are usually not good things. It takes your planning and strategizing to overcome every negative thing that may want to hinder your targets from becoming fully achieved. Learn to work with God and mentors to develop and finalize your strategies.

3. **Improve yourself**. Your capacity in the previous year maybe inadequate to achieve the targets of a new year. Build your capacity muscles to excel. This may require you buying new books, watching new documentaries, attending trainings and seminars, or just sitting down to think. But by all means, build your capacity to achieve your targets through your strategies.

4. **Take control**. Take control of your life and strategies/ targets. Going to work, and doing the work are not the same. Step up your game and take full responsibility. Be in-charge, plan your time, day, month or year, and take absolute control of your life and work.

5. **Learn from your supervisors/superiors.** Many staff are comfortable doing the same thing repeatedly, the same way and with the same mistakes. Many of us have become complacent, waiting for our supervisors to nudge us to do better. This may never happen, and even if it happens, it may happen too late. Training and mentorship are ongoing activities every day and every time. Use every opportunity you have to assess and learn from your supervisors and superiors. Ask yourself: Is my report clearly presented and on time? Do(es) my weekly goal(s) have a clear point? Is the work I'm doing engaging enough? What have I learnt from my supervisor/superiors in the past one week?

If the answer to any of these questions is "nothing!" change your approach immediately.

6. **Sit at your desk.** Most staff use field works to deny themselves the benefits of sitting at their desk. For instance, field work is great. However, office work is essential. It is the work in the office that makes the field work seamless. Until you sit down to think and strategize, you will struggle and sweat in the field. Staying all day outside the office leads to struggle in the field. Do not use field work as an excuse not to work at your desk. Many do their own things and claim they are working in the field. It always shows with time!

7. **Adjust your attention span and work harder.** You may be used to getting what you want in a few minutes (10 – 30 minutes). Maybe in school, classes were even shortened with all manner of interludes. Re-train your attention span to process long—very long. Time waits for no one. Learn to work longer and harder. It takes smart-hard work to overcome poverty and become prosperous. Learn to work hard and smart.

8. **Get results, don't just Work.** Most of the real work is done outside the work hours. Rule of thumb: one hour of work requires two hours of preparation. Block out the times of the week when you will just think, prepare and study. Have a self-defined thinking time! Above all, do not count the number of hours you have put into the work as the real deal – count the number of work packages you have completed within the period. It is the products (results) that matter, not just the process.

9. **Deliver your work packages.** Much valuable time is lost doing what you like, rather than what you are asked to do. Supervisors go to great lengths to craft

appropriate work packages (and sub-work packages), and expect head-on responses to exactly what they asked. Stay focused, stay committed and work diligently. If confused, ask questions. It is always good to know what is expected as early as possible, than to rework an already completed work because the process or product was wrong.

10. **Read through each work package three times.** Before you begin to respond to a work package, construct an inception report that shows how well you understood the assignment. Then read your inception report three times before commencing the work. When you finish the task, check if your inception report is still valid. When you get comments from your supervisor, go through thoroughly, and learn from the review process. Making the same mistake twice shows inability to learn.

11. **Connect with your supervisor/mentors.** The single most underutilized resource at work place is the office hours, now available in-person, by e-mail, or by Skype. You might not have realized it, but your supervisors/ mentors are in their offices just to meet with you and help you with your work package(s). Your work may come out better if you have a chance to ask questions on grey areas that are not very clear. Connect to collect!

12. **Pursue your passion.** Amidst all the work packages, general office demands and requirements, and must-do from your supervisors, it's easy to forget what your real interests, gifts, and passions are in the first place. Each month, be sure to take out time to do something you're good at and are really interested in. The joy of doing something you enjoy—and doing it well—will go a long

way to making up for all the unpleasant things you have to do at work.

13. **Regularly evaluate your target.** You must do a regular check-up on your targets and evaluate progress towards your goals. To ensure continual improvement, your plan must be revisited and evaluated. You should ask yourself questions like: Are you still working with the strategy you planned to use to achieve the targets – for your career, academics, finances, family, social life, spirituality, and community development? How do you measure the progress recorded?

14. **Delay gratification.** According to Wikipedia, delayed gratification is the ability to resist the temptation for an immediate reward and wait for a later reward. Generally, delayed gratification is associated with resisting a smaller but more immediate reward in order to receive a larger or more enduring reward later. Do you want to be successful in your career, relationship and all areas where you have set targets for the year? Then you must learn to delay gratification.

15. **Reward yourself.** Create a reward system for yourself. If you have done well, you should reward yourself for doing well. You can get lost in the search for something better that you forget to give yourself a pat on the back for all the good things you have already achieved. Get a journal and record your successes and remember to reward yourself.

CHAPTER 38

WHY ASK

Sometimes we feel it is better to keep our mouths shut and not ask for anything because we don't want to disturb our friends, spouse, parents or even God. We think it is gentlemanly or lady-like not to ask. Some people pride themselves by saying "I don't ask anybody for anything." It's like a label, "I'm sufficient in myself". Even if they don't have, they don't like asking people for anything.

Matthew 7:7-8 *"Ask and it will be given to you; seek and you will find; knock and the door will be opened to you. ⁸ For everyone who asks receives; the one who seeks finds; and to the one who knocks, the door will be opened.*

Until we ask, we are not qualified to receive. Until we knock, the doors will not be opened unto us. Until we seek, we may never find any good thing. So, living your life without asking, seeking and knocking is actually denying yourself access to what you should have received, what you should have found, and doors that should have been opened to you. The question is not whether we should ask, seek or knock, but who should we ask? From whom should we seek? And which doors should we knock? It is important that you learn to ask God, people and yourself questions at strategic points in your life.

In verse 11, it says, *if ye then, being evil, know how to give good gifts unto your children, how much more shall your Father which is in heaven give good things to them that ask him?*

Until you ask, He will not give you anything. God is a good God. He gives gifts to everyone, but He does not give good gifts just to those He loves or those who are born again or those that go to church, but primarily to those that ask. There are many things that can never come to you except you ask Him. There are many good things you will not find unless you seek them, and there are many doors that will never open unless you knock on them. So, it is important that you understand that your destiny is largely your mouth determined. The Bible says, a man shall eat good by the fruits of his lips. Asking is a critical divine and spiritual channel for God's blessings. Some of us will be praying some beautiful prayers and disturbing heaven, when actually God says, just ask. Learn to ask Him in line with the scriptures.

Jeremiah 33:3 says; *Call unto me, and I will answer thee, and shew thee great and mighty things, which thou knowest not.*

Until you ask, He will not show you anything. Our walk with God is a work of a son or daughter and a Father. Just like our children keep asking us all manner of things – food, school fees, snacks, toys, play time, cloths, holidays, etc; or question us about things and issues of life, and we patiently answer them; God also expects you and I to ask him all sorts of questions. Don't close your mouth, just ask. Let it be that you asked and He didn't give to you, than possibly missing out of all you would have had if you only you asked.

In life, God answers us in different ways. You may ask and He will say yes, take or have it; or you may ask and He says no; or you may ask and he says wait. But ask. Don't assume. If you are single and see a lady/man you like, please be bold enough to ask - are you married, engaged or available. Ask questions. Also, in your life, ask questions; in your career, ask questions; and in your finances, ask questions. It is good to sit down once in a while and ask yourselves some very hard questions. What can I do better? How can I improve myself? How can I be a better individual? How can I live a better life? How can I change the way things are happening around me? Ask questions.

Don't ask God "why" but ask Him "how". Or ask Him; "what will you have me do?", How do I achieve what you want me to achieve?" "What do I have to do that will enable me acquire a mega testimony that will announce me?" When you go to work on Monday morning, sit behind your desk for 5 minutes, ask yourself, "What must I achieve this week?" "What must I deliver before Wednesday?" "What are the critical job tasks I must achieve and be satisfied that this week has not been wasted?"

It is one thing to come to work, but a completely different thing to achieve results. Reflect on this: "What can I do that by this time next year I will have better results?" Do not make your failure everybody's failure. Everyone is different. If you are doing well, you will know; and if you are not doing well, you will also know. Be honest with yourself. Don't allow people's opinions to decide your destiny. Ask yourself, "What can I do to be better?" "What can I do to improve myself?" When you begin to believe that everybody is not doing well, then you have missed it.

Understand that destinies are **Unique, Private and Personal.**

CHAPTER 39

BORROW TO SUCCEED

I know many of us have been advised not to borrow. This advice may come from well-meaning friends, families and even our pastors. In most churches, it is described as anti-covenant to borrow. Allow me to surprise you. **It is covenant and acceptable to borrow.** It is Biblical too. Borrowing may appear unconventional, but it is approved by God as it is one of the divine avenues available to help believers succeed. Now before you get me wrong, follow me and let us take a walk.

2 Kings 4:1-3: *Now there cried a certain woman of the wives of the sons of the prophets unto Elisha, saying, thy servant my husband is dead; and thou knowest that thy servant did fear the LORD: and the creditor is come to take unto him my two sons to be bondmen. ² And Elisha said unto her, what shall I do for thee? Tell me, what hast thou in the house? And she said, thine handmaid hath not anything in the house, save a pot of oil. ³ Then he said, go, borrow thee vessels abroad of all thy neighbours, even empty vessels; borrow not a few.*

There are two kinds of borrowing – borrowing to succeed or borrowing to die. Let me begin by explaining the second type of borrowing – borrowing to die.

Every time you borrow to eat, buy new clothes, shoes, pay house rent, school fees, or buy car for personal use, you are killing your destiny consciously. This must be what the prophet did that led to his death. The covenant is against you borrowing – like the prophet – to meet daily needs. This kills and should be completely avoided in life and ministry.

However, you can borrow to succeed. Our success begins from what we know we have (she had oil in the house). You have gifts, talents, abilities and even resources in you and around you. That is the starting point of your miracles. No one can ever be successful without first identifying the resources which can be developed. Every creature of God has something – and these divine gifts vary from persons to persons. Your success in life begins with you recognizing what you have.

To succeed, you may have to borrow what you do not have. This widow would have lost her two children if she did not follow the simple instruction to borrow. There are five things you may have to borrow to succeed in life;

1. **Stories: Borrow other people's stories**. Listen to the stories of men and learn from them. A wise man said there are three ways to learn in life; by observation, instruction, and experience. Friends, experience is the worst teacher as sometimes you may never recover from it. Listen to the stories of men and learn from

them. Borrow their testimonies, borrow the stories of how they overcame life challenges and encounters they had, borrow their mistakes, experiences and avoid them, borrow their breakthroughs and do what they did to advance your life.

2. **Strategies: Borrow other people's strategies**. Sir Isaac Newton once said "If I have seen further than others, it is by standing on the shoulders of giants." Have mentors and borrow their strategies. It is madness trying to re-invent the wheel; it is senseless wasting your whole life trying to discover what has already been discovered. Find out what other people are doing to succeed and follow their steps, it is the easiest way to succeed. Again, you don't need to make the same mistakes your father made in the past. Learn from them and use existing successful strategies to escape them. You should freely borrow other people's strategies, but if you need to pay for them, please do.

3. **Skills: Borrow skills**. In life, you may not be able to execute your vision and mission all by yourself. Borrow the skills of people. Do not borrow just any skills, borrow relevant value adding skills. You should not waste your resources on irrelevant skills. It will be difficult to teach an eagle how to swim but you can teach an eagle to fly better. Also, do not try to do everything – borrow to stay focused on where you have strength and comparative advantage.

4. **Solutions: Borrow the solutions of others**. There is nothing new under the sun. Everything you set out to do has been done by someone before. Just copy, adapt and paste – and acknowledge the source. You are permitted to borrow the solutions developed by

others. You know why the woman saved her children? It is because she found out that Elisha had provided solution to the problem of others in Chapter 2 of 2Kings (vs19-22) when the water in the land was full of death, he healed the waters. She believed that he too can solve her problems.

5. **Resources**: Borrow resources including money to succeed. A friend said, borrowing is like using the money that you do not have now but will have, to create the future you do not have but desire to have. Borrow to start your business, borrow to bring your inventions to light, borrow, to open up new opportunities, borrow to execute a business deal including contracts, borrow to enhance your liquidity and improve your solvency. Borrow to ensure better results and outcomes. Borrow money, people, tools, equipment, offices, etc., to ensure proper take off, continuity and completion of project. Borrow, not a few!

If you must succeed in life, I ask that you set out deliberately and consciously to borrow stories, strategies, skills, solutions and resources that you need to change ranks. It is biblical, acceptable and it is expected. The worst thing you can do to yourself is to borrow money to eat, buy clothes or shoes which is what the bible says you shouldn't do.

In business if you borrow other people's money, it is acceptable, it is called OPM (Other People's Money). Most of the wealthiest people in our times will not be where they are if they did not take bank loans. Today, Dangote of Nigeria is building a refinery that will cost him billions of dollars. He could not afford it on his own; he had to borrow to make it happen. Bill Gate borrowed to start Microsoft. Show me a very successful business man, and I am sure that somewhere in his/her rise, they took loans. And they are still borrowing peoples' skills to stay alive.

Jesus borrowed Peter's boat to preach the Beatitudes, borrowed fish and bread to feed the 5000 and 4000 people. He also borrowed an ass to ride into Jerusalem. He even borrowed the grave where he was buried. But after feeding the 5,000 he returned 12 baskets to the boy (profit of the investment made). Without the boy's input, there would have been no 12 leftover baskets. Sometimes, you are allowed to borrow, but borrow the right things and for the right purposes.

CHAPTER 40

CONFRONT YOUR LIONS

There are many lions on our path to victory and success in life. We must begin, and be willing to confront them. In Judges 14 Samson saw a young lady in Philistines and wanted to marry her. His father and mother were against the idea initially, but they came to terms with it and agreed to support him. As they took steps to marry the girl, a lion emerged and roared!

Judges 14:5:

⁵ Then went Samson down, and his father and his mother, to Timnath, and came to the vineyards of Timnath: and, behold, a young lion roared against him.

Every time you are on the path to greatness, fulfillment of visions, and realization of dreams; there are lions. We see lions in every man's journey of life. If you have not met any, you will meet one soon - I assure you. Lions are real, and I mean, roaring lions. Your lion could be financial issues, family crisis, bad friends, debts, an associate or colleagues in the office. Your behavior, characters, bad habits you want to stop but cannot stop like smoking, drinking, etc. could also be your lions. It is important to understand that obstacles in your path way to success are called lions.

Normally, any natural man could have turned back and ran from the lion to save his life. Even an English adage says "He that fights and runs away, lives to fight another day". But that was not what Samson did. He did the opposite. He stood his ground and confronted his lion. Since June 2014, I have had to confront many lions. Today, I am a far better person than I was then. Friends, confront your lions. Murmuring over your lions will not help you. Running from them is not better. Samson confronted the lion roaring at him, and even killed it with bare hands. You don't need heavy equipment/gadgets to confront your lions.

See what happened in verses 8-9; *⁸ After some time, when he returned to get her, he turned aside to see the carcass of the lion. And behold, a swarm of bees and honey were in the carcass of the lion. ⁹ He took some of it in his hands and went along, eating. When he came to his father and mother, he gave some to them, and they also ate. But he did not tell them that he had taken the honey out of the carcass of the lion.*

He ate honey from the same lion that tried to stop him. And even gave some to his parents. What is the lesion in this? Your blessing(s) is/are wrapped around lions. The sweetness you want in your live is wrapped around the lion roaring at you now. Running from the lion is losing the opportunity of having an enjoyable life. When you refuse to confront your lions, you lose opportunities in life.

There are several lions you must confront in your life journey; and in confronting them you are qualified and empowered to eat the honey in them. It is time to confront your lions. Don't just sit down and say next year I am going to do this or do that. Confront them from now. I may not know what your lion(s) is/are. Yours may be a broken relationship, a financial hardship, career challenges and or crisis, etc. To scale new heights, you MUST confront your lions!

You may be asking me, what does it take to confront my lion? Allow me to give you five (5) basic steps to confronting your lions;

1. ***Believe in yourself:*** Samson confronted the lion because he believed in himself. He had no weapons. He destroyed the lion with his bare hands! His belief in himself killed the lion. I knew some people who have spent more than six years for their doctoral degree, but I spent only 2 years. Why? I confronted the lions. Believe in yourself. If you don't believe in yourself, no one will believe in you. Don't wait for anyone to build your ego, build your own ego. Believe that anything is doable, you can overcome it. Speak to your ego - I can achieve this. Confront that lion.

2. ***Engage your mind:*** Your mind is the power house of your destiny. You need to sit down and think on how you want to overcome your lion. It is not just by

physical strength, life is not about exerting physical strength, it is about exerting first mental strength from your mind. It is about taking intelligent steps. The Bible says, "as a man thinketh in his heart so is he" (Proverbs 23:7). Put your mind to work. For many of us, our minds are redundant. As long as you don't engage your mind, you will waste away in life. The difference between one successful man and another is the mind impact resulting from mind engagement. *If your mind is not engaged, no one will mind you.*

3. ***Depend on the Spirit of God.*** And the Spirit of the LORD came mightily upon him (verse 6), and he tore the lion apart. No one has the power to handle a lion alone. Partnership with God is an amazing success strategy. You may think that you have all that it takes, but friend, you need God in your life. Work with the Spirit, move with the Spirit, listen to the guidance of the Spirit, and you will be amazed at your result.

4. ***Be careful with whom you share your testimony with:*** Despite his victory, the Bible said, *"But he did not tell them that he had taken the honey out of the carcass of the lion".(Verse 9).* He did not tell his father or his mother that he killed a lion. And when he told his girlfriend, he was put into troubles. Be mindful of who you share your testimony with, because in the journey of life there are vision killers, vision stealers, vision destroyers and vision enablers. Ensure that you are talking with enablers of your vision, not the killer of your vision. And finally,

5. ***Evaluate yourself****: After some time, when he returned to get her, he turned aside to see the carcass of the lion. And behold, a swarm of bees and honey were in the carcass of the lion. (Verse 8).* If Samson had disappeared after killing the lion and never returned to look at it again, he would have laboured in vain. At the end of every day, ask yourself, "What did I plan to achieve this day that I did not achieve? How can I make it better tomorrow?" Begin now to organize yourself; nothing happens on its own - you must work it out. No matter how good your plan is, if you don't work it out, it can never work. What do I need to do differently tomorrow that will give me a better return by end of the month, year or even next year? He returned to the carcass and he found the honey.

Therefore, confront the lions of your destiny. It could be laziness, idleness, sluggishness, procrastinations, bad habit, bad character, wrong friends, etc. There are many lions of destiny! It could even be negligence in doing your work, poor time management with shabby results. If you are not growing, it is your choice. Read, study and learn. There are free courses you can find online and register such as Coursera, Alison, edX, Skillshare etc. You can learn new skills from these platforms and grow. Learn how to negotiate business, how to run systems free of charge. Never waste another day, confront your lions now.

CHAPTER 41

WHY DO WE PRAY?

A wise man once said "when purpose is unknown abuse is inevitable." Once in a while, we should remind ourselves of the reasons why we pray, especially as we scale new heights.

1Corinthians 15:57

⁵⁷ *But thanks be to God, which giveth us the victory through our Lord Jesus Christ.*

Victory in life is not a function of our qualification, but a function of our connection to the source of victory. Jesus Christ came, died for us, that we may have access to the God of victory - Jehovah. The Bible says, thanks be to God in heaven who gives us victory through his son Jesus Christ. He gives us victory in our family lives, academics, work places, finances, investments, and health etc. Truly, all round victory comes from above.

James 1:17

17 Every good gift and every perfect gift is from above, and cometh down from the Father of lights, with whom is no variableness, neither shadow of turning.

Friends, victory in every area of life comes from above. That you are alive and strong is not because you are special or know it all, it is because there is victory in God through Jesus Christ our Lord. Understanding this will humble you. Many of us are so proud of what we have achieved and who we think we are. Friends, we are not achievers. We are mere receivers of His grace and helps. The Bible says, "what do we have that we have not received" (1 Corinthians 4:7). If you have received everything from him, why act like you did it by your own power? You will be amazed to find out that the things that matter to you were divinely orchestrated. Was it you that made youself who you are today? Every victory we have in life came from God, and if we fail to understand this, we may end up losing God's involvement in our lives. If we do not acknowledge him daily in prayers, we can offend him. It is harmful not to be grateful. Also, our level of gratitude to God determines our altitude from Him.

Why else must we connect to this God regularly?

Job 9:10

10 Which doeth great things past finding out; yea, and wonders without number.

If it is wonderful, it is God-full. If anything you see is wonderful, then it is from the God that does wonders without numbers. If what you want is great, then you need the great God.

What therefore are we supposed to do to enjoy these wonders without numbers?

Great worship, great appreciation and great dependency on him to deliver great wonders in our lives. Hear this advice from Paul to the Corinthians as recorded in *1Corinthians 15:58*

⁵⁸ Therefore, my beloved brethren, be ye steadfast, unmovable, always abounding in the work of the Lord, forasmuch as ye know that your labour is not in vain in the Lord.

Be steadfast: A double minded man is unstable in all his ways (James 1:8). What qualifies you for victory in God is your stability and immovability. Do not be a know it all, being everywhere. Be unmovable. For any big truck to be able to move something, it must be stable. Your stability is important for you to enjoy the various victories you desire from God. If your eyes be single, your body will be full of light. This connotes stability.

Get to a point in life where you just know what you want in life and stick with it. Steve Jobs said "know what you want to do in life and stay in it." The God we have connected to is the God that doeth great things, wonders without numbers. This is why we pray, because we are looking up to God and our victory is in him through Christ Jesus. Our

God does uncountable wonders. He is not tired of doing wonders – even in your life.

My prayer for you this year is that this wonder working God will surprise you. This year only victory will be our portion. Praying with fasting makes tremendous power available and fast tracks destines. ***So, why fast again?

CHAPTER 42

WHY FAST AGAIN?

We all know the story of David. He went into Bathsheba, the wife of Uriah the Hittite, got her pregnant, killed her husband, and married her. God told him through Prophet Nathan that what he did was wrong. When the baby was born, the child became sick and David fasted day and night for God's forgiveness and asked God to preserve the life of the baby. But the baby died.

When the baby died, his servants and men were afraid to tell him as they were scared, he will hurt or even kill himself. But when he learned of the child's death, he stopped fasting. When his men wanted to know why, he said,

*But now he is dead, **wherefore should I fast?** Can I bring him back again? I shall go to him, but he shall not return to me (2Samuel 12:23).*

When people fast and pray, but don't get what they want from God the way they wanted it, when asked to fast and pray again, they complain by asking, "What I asked God to do the last time, He didn't do it; Wherefore should I fast?", "I fasted for 21 days last year and asked God for just one thing, and He didn't do it, wherefore should I fast?". People come up with all manner of excuses why they should not fast regularly.

A lot of us feel there is no reason to fast or pray again since we haven't seen the results of past prayers. The question before us today is, why fast again?

1. **Fasting Saves You Money**: Most fasting and prayer time covers breakfast and lunch, so money is saved. If nothing else, fasting saves you money. The resources you would have used to buy food is saved; the time you would have used to prepare breakfast and lunch is saved and can be invested towards other profitable ventures. Yes, fasting saves you money.

2. **Medically, Fasting is Very Healthy**. It makes you lose weight, purges/cleans your system, and help eliminate free radicals. It keeps you healthy. One of the easiest ways of getting our organs to function better is by fasting. Most times our systems are over burdened with all manner of things, but when we fast, we give our organs time to clear out things, relax and recuperate. Medically speaking, science has shown that fasting is very healthy as organs and systems recover from toxins and begin to function optimally.

3. **Spiritually, Fasting Brings You Nearer to God**: Understand that fasting does not bring God nearer to you, rather it brings you nearer to GOD! This is,

however, achieved when we truly fast and are not just on a hunger strike. That you don't have food in your house and then decide to fast is not real fasting. Fasting is when there is a lot of food in your house or you have the capacity to buy food, but you consciously decide to abstain.

4. **Seeking better things:** In Ezra, 8:21: ... *to seek of him a straight way for us.* We fast for personal goals. We fast to seek divine direction, divine guidance and divine leadings. We fast to seek God's face and to ask Him what next we must do, and how to go about it? It is a period of seeking divine guidance. It is the time to tell God all that we have done that has not worked and enquire on what next He would have us do. Fasting presents a unique and golden opportunity to seek God for our career breakthroughs, marital breakthroughs, family breakthroughs, financial breakthroughs, fruitfulness, health and healing, etc. It is an opportunity to seek God for yourself.

5. **Seeking for Divine Direction**...*that we may seek him and ask him for a right way for us.* In the world today, there are several ways but only one right way; there are several men, but only one right man for you; several women, but only one right woman for you; several jobs, but only one right job for you; and several places, but only one right place at any point in time. The truth remains that only God knows the right way, the right person, the right job or the right place. So, we seek Him to access the right way. He told Peter after His resurrection in John 21:6 to cast his net on the right side. There is a right side to

everything in life. You only have knowledge of and access to the right side when you seek God. There is a kind of blessing, breakthrough, or victory you cannot enjoy except by prayer and fasting. There are a number of things in me and in you that cannot go out except we fast and pray.

6. **Welfare of our children and posterity:** *....and for our little ones (Vs 21).* We also fast for our children and children's children (i.e. our posterity). We fast for posterity, for our little ones, for our children even the ones yet unborn. If you do not begin right now to pray for them and bestow upon them what you want, they may become problems for you in the future. Concerning Abraham, the Bible said that he paid tithe for Levi while he was still in the womb (Hebrew 7:9). No wonder he later became the priest and was receiving tithe of all. In one of my courses, I discovered that children in a lady's womb were actually formed in their grandmother's womb. So, you have a mandate from God to fast and pray for your little children.

7. **Provisions and prosperity:** *...and for all our substances (Vs 21).*We must also fast for our substances. Everybody has prosperity needs. Poverty is a curse. Believing and waiting for God to change our status is wasting. We fast to change our financial levels. Fasting is the easiest way to work in prosperity following seed sown. Fasting puts you in the fast tract of life as it flattens your tummy, but fattens your pockets. Fasting flourishes people's destinies. Fasting breaks the yoke and curse of poverty and delivers prosperity to the individual...

and many actually save a lot of resources during fasting from food not eaten and this could be invested as seeds for wealth.

8. **For Answered prayers...**"*So we fasted and besought our God for this; and He was intreated of us (Vs 23).*" This is our confidence – that God will move on our behalf.

True fasting has three main components:

- Self-denial – this could be from food, sex, or other things you love and enjoy;
- Prayers for yourself, others, the kingdom and the nation; and
- Giving of alms to the needy and destitute in your community. Doing good to people, community and nation is a vital component of fasting. True fasting is, therefore, not complete until you miss something that you love so much, pray to God and give something to someone who needs it. This is what Isaiah 58:6 – 12 called the chosen fast.

Is not this the fast that I have chosen? To loose the bands of wickedness, to undo the heavy burdens, and to let the oppressed go free, and that ye break every yoke? **Isaiah 58:6**

If you have never consciously given out something that is tangible while fasting, then try to do so during your next season of fasting.

7 Is it not to deal thy bread to the hungry, and that thou bring the poor that are cast out to thy house? When thou seest the naked, that thou cover him; and that thou hide not thyself from thine own flesh? (Isaiah 58:7)

Plan for it so that you do not give excuses while it was never done. Go to schools, churches, destitute, and orphanages. Pay children's school fees, repair structures, help somebody, feed the hungry, support the motherless, and if possible, give shelter to the homeless. Your fasting is never complete until something leaves you to someone.

Why fast again? It is commanded. It is a time of reflection. I recently read a book from a great author on leadership. Every year or quarter he recommends you go on a personal retreat for 2 or more days and reflect on your life. If you cannot do it every quarter, reflect on yourself at least once every year. Ask yourself, "What have I done so far with my life? What am I going to do now?" Do not allow the year to just pass you by without reflecting to make your year a productive one.

Discipline, dedication, and commitment are required to succeed in a fast.

CHAPTER 43

BE-FRIEND AND UN-FRIEND

There are people around us that occupy the space, but add no value to our lives. How many of us are in such a position where we have so many friends who are not adding values or making any difference in our lives? If a lock has a key in it, another key may not enter into it because it is occupied. So many of us have our lives occupied by the wrong friends and the good ones cannot come in. I say to you right now "be-friend and un-friend".

Proverbs 27:17: *Iron sharpeneth iron; so a man sharpeneth the countenance of his friend.*

True friends do not just stay and occupy space, they add values! The Bible declares *"Iron sharpeneth iron; so a man sharpeneth the countenance of his friend."* The number of people adding value to you will tell you how many friends you truly have. "He/she is my friend." Anyone can say that. But what relevance are you bringing to that relationship? Relationships are only meaningful if there is an element of relevance.

A man marries a wife and she becomes a part of his household. That woman will add value to the man and the man to the woman for the friendship to continue. This is the only way to avoid problems. It is good to have many people following you on Facebook, Twitter, LinkedIn, etc. But how many are your true friends? Many of us have so many friends but are still lonely! This is the hard truth. Our relationships will determine how well we are.

David and Jonathan were friends, and together they helped each other. Amnon and Jonadab were also friends, and together they destroyed each other. Befriend and unfriend.

Why must you befriend and unfriend?

1. **Life is meaningless without *good* friends**: Man was created to have friends. You can't afford to live in isolation. Bible says woe to him that stands alone. (Ecclesiastes 4:9-12). Jesus Christ was never alone while on earth. He had the 3, 12, 70 and 120. The son of God needed people around him. Even God was never alone from the beginning. In the book of Genesis, he said "Let us make man in our own image" (Genesis 1:26), meaning he was not alone. He had a company around him. The angels go in groups "the host of angels". The time God sent Angel Gabriel alone to bring a result to Daniel (Daniel 10:12-13), he couldn't make it. The prince of Persia held him back for 21 days until Angel Michael came to support him. Friends, it is dangerous to live alone. Everyone needs a friend. Irrespective of your age, status, position or race, you need friends.

Running your life in isolation - think alone, eat alone, make money and spend it alone, live alone, work alone - is very dangerous. If you do not show up at work and no one calls to ask after you (not just the HR, but someone who cares), then there is a big problem. Friends, life is programmed for friendship.

2. **Life is destroyed by *wrong* friendship**: Life is programmed for friendship, but is also destroyed by wrong friends. When you enclose yourself with wrong people, they can easily destroy your life or mortgage your destiny. Most people are destroyed by peer influence. If you have the wrong kinds of friends, they can use you for all manner of things. People have gone to parties with their 'friends' and never came back! People are drug addicts, drunkards, prostitutes, or even armed robbers today because of their 'friends'. Be careful. Many have followed their so-called friends and ended up in prisons, detention camps or in chains. Think, review and analyse before joining your life with anybody.

3. **You can handle a certain number of friends at any given point in time**: At any given point in time in life, there is a limit to the number of friends you can effectively handle – this is what I call the **Friendship Limit**. When that number is reached, you cannot accommodate any more friend. Woe betides you if you have your friendship quota filled with the wrong kind of friends. Remember the case of Solomon's son Rehoboam who filled his life with wrong friends, took their counsel and eventually lost his kingdom (1Kings 12:3-20).

4. **Our destinies are determined by the friends we keep**: A wise man said "show me your friend and I will tell you who you are". Your friends can attract blessings or curses to you. Consciously look for friends that will attract blessings, favours and good to you, and join yourself to them.

You may all be at the same level right now, but shortly, everyone's level will change. There are factors that will separate one from another, and one of these factors is who you are following - Elisha followed Elijah and his life changed. What value are your friends adding to your life? Also, what value are you adding to others?

Receive grace from God to be-friend and un-friend the wrong ones in Jesus name.

CHAPTER 44

THOU SHALL OWE – GOD'S COMMANDMENT TO OWE!

God commands us to owe! I am so sure that you are amazed by this statement. Friends, owing is a divine commandment. Whether we know it or not, we are debtors. But what does the bible command us to owe? What is this debt universally commanded by God?

Romans 13:8: Owe no man anything, but to love one another: for he that loveth another hath fulfilled the law.

The primary and only approved debt we owe people is love. If you constantly pay this debt, you have fulfilled the law. No wonder the Bible declares that loving God and man with all your heart, mind and soul is the summary of the whole law and its fulfilment. The idea of living for yourself and by yourself is against the law. We are forever in debt. You owe everyone around you a debt of love!

You get love by loving others, you get happy by making others happy, and you obtain mercy by being merciful to others. This is why I strongly believe in the three S of life – seed, sacrifice and service.

Therefore, when people complain that nobody likes them – if you check very well, you will discover that they are victims of their own seeds. When you truly fail to like people, people will consciously refuse you; when you choose not to care for others, people will deny you their care. To the merciful, God shall show himself merciful. It is what you sow, that you reap. That is why the Golden Rule stipulates, "Do unto others as thou would like them to do unto you." If you want to reap happiness, then sow happiness. If you want to reap joy, sow joy. If you want people to care for you, care for others. If you want people to give to you, give to others. As long as you do not understand this simple biblical principle, life will remain a burden to you. I do not care how much you have/do not have, I care about what you do with what you have. Do not forget Galatians 6:7

Be not deceived; God is not mocked: for whatsoever a man soweth, that shall he also reap.

If you sow love, you would reap love, if you sow hatred, you would reap plenty of hatred. A man once told me that women are multipliers. If you give them joy, they multiply it. Likewise, if its hatred you gave them, they do deliver multiples. So is the principle of life: whatever you give to anyone is multipliable. That is why you are forever indebted – for your own good.

Every day and every month of your life, ask yourself this simple question: "have I paid my debt of love, my debt of care, of making people happy, of distributing myself? If the answer is no, know that your debt is increasing. It is critical that we understand this debt. One of the easiest ways of paying this debt is in Job 42:10

And the Lord turned the captivity of Job, when he prayed for his friends: also the Lord gave Job twice as much as he had before.

One of the easiest ways of showing you love someone is to sit down and pray for that person. If someone is going through a challenge, rather than mocking and jesting, sit down and pray for that person. Sit down and pray that God shall see this person through whatever they are passing through. When someone is having issues in life, do not use it as a gossip topic, pray for that person. Because in praying for that person, you are paying your debt of love.

Some years ago, when my first son was born, I was in Abuja. Same day he was born, I was working hard to save the life of a woman who was in labour and had no money to pay in my private facility. Little did I know that my own wife was in the same condition somewhere in Port Harcourt. That was her first pregnancy and nurses were on strike. The few nurses present at the University Clinic, where she went for a check-up rejected her. The nurses had already agreed that they will not have her admitted nor deliver there but a nursed asked that they first examine her. Upon examination, she was found to be far gone into labour. They changed their views and allowed her to be admitted and deliver there – as sending her away at that stage was dangerous. I had no idea all of this was going on as I was struggling to save the life of someone else's wife and child. Do not be deceived, God is not mocked, for whatever seed a man sows, that, he shall reap.

Friends, life is a product of the seeds that we sow and the time we invest. Seed time and harvest time shall not cease. Learn therefore to pay your love debt daily, weekly, monthly and yearly; and as you do this, the best of God shall come our way.

CHAPTER 45

BE ACCOUNTABLE

I asked my staff the benefits of accountability and below are some of their comments;

1. It builds confidence;
2. It builds trust;
3. It is a check and balance for responsibility;
4. It makes you spend well;
5. It makes you disciplined;
6. It gives a control;
7. It helps you measure your success;
8. It helps in monitoring and evaluation;
9. It makes you standout; and
10. It makes you manage better

Everything listed above are benefits of accountability but there is one that is not commonly known to people or discussed. I will focus on this other benefit of accountability – preservation of life and destines.

1kings 20:39-40.

[39] *As the king passed by, the prophet called out to him, "Your servant went into the thick of the battle, and someone came to me with a captive and said, 'Guard this man. If he is missing, it will be your life for his life, or you must pay a talent[a] of silver.'* **[40]** *While your servant was busy here and there, the man disappeared." "That is your sentence," the king of Israel said. "You have pronounced it yourself."*

Accountability preserves destinies. Accountability preserves careers, life, marriage, finances, health, and anything around you. It preserves your ministry and your future. Hear this servant, *"As your servant was busy here and there…."* He was busy. He was not idle, yet he lost it. Being busy does not mean being in business. Being busy does not equate to doing the right thing. For instance, that you come to work by 7.00 or 8.00 am, and remain busy all day, does not mean you achieved anything. Actually, if you achieved anything, it was either using, spending, or at worse wasting the time you had to invest and change your life.

People may truly be busy, very busy, and yet not be able to make any impact. Chatting on WhatsApp, Facebook, etc. or listening to music, watching a sermon, or even providing counselling to somebody are all good – but if these hinders you from achieving the goals of your organization, meeting your daily targets, or delaying your team's submission, then you are not doing well. Please remember that there is a TIME FOR EVERTHING UNDER HEAVEN – said the very wise man, Solomon (Ecclesiastes 3:1).

It is, therefore, important that we build into our lives the culture of **accountability**. However, it requires that you accept responsibility to become accountable in life. Many consciously or otherwise project their responsibilities to others – it is their fault. Have you not heard people say commonly, it is my father's, my mother's, my cousin's, my uncle's or even teacher's, friend's, peer's fault? Have you not heard them say "people I believed in, trusted, depended on or even worked for, failed me? Dear, until you take responsibility, you cannot be accountable, and until you are accountable, the situation will never change. Please understand this moment that you are **FULLY** accountable and responsible for whatever has happened or is happening to you. Until you accept this truth, your redemption is far, if not impossible. Many have lost their businesses, careers, homes, families, marriages, and all things that are important to them by not being accountable. Be accountable.

Account for every minute you spend in the office and outside the office; account for every kobo that enters your bank account; and account for every meeting you attend and what value(s) you add. Be accountable to yourself, your family, your friends and your employers. When you begin to account for anything and everything that happens to you, preservation becomes the order of the day. I do not necessarily mean that you must write them down on paper (that may be useful), but please be always conscious of every hour, minute, and second that you spend. Be conscious of everything you say to your friends, colleagues, spouse, parents, etc. Be accountable for all your actions and inactions.

Here are three fundamental requirements for accountability;

1. **Focus:** You cannot be accountable except you are focused. Strive to focus on what you want to do, what you have purposed to do, and whatever you are assigned to do. Your focus is a primary requirement for accountability. The Bible speaking on focus said, – "… if therefore thine eye be single, thy whole body shall be full of light."(Matthew 6:22).

2. **Keep the Price and Prize of Accountability in View**: While the price refers to the cost of accountability or not being accountable on you, your family or the organization; the prize could be a punishment (for not being accountable) or a reward (for being very accountable). Some mistakes are very costly to the individual, family or organization where you work. Also, do not always assume that you will go free for not being accountable. That you escaped the punishment of not being accountable before does not mean you will always escape. Keep the price and prize in view (1Corinthians 9:24, Philippians 3:14)

3. **Remember there is ALWAYS the Day of Judgment**: For every assignment entrusted to you, there is a day of evaluation – a day when your acts shall be brought to light and you will be measured based on what you have done. It may not be a physical measurement, it may not be your boss measuring your work, it may not be your organization, husband or your wife, but the day will always come. It could even be you measuring your work and asking yourself probing questions. There is always a time of judgment, a day of evaluation, a day when your results shall be reviewed (2Peter 2:9).

CHAPTER 46

THE POWER OF REVIEW

In **Ezra 8:1-14, we** have a line-up of men and women that went up with Ezra when they had a mandate – they went in multitudes. *Verse 15 says*; and *I gathered them together to the river that runneth to Ahava; and there abode we in tents three days: and I viewed the people, and the priests, and found there none of the sons of Levi.*

Multiple does not always mean completeness. Having multiple does not mean the person that you need most is around you. For the single boy or single girl; having multiple people asking you for marriage does not mean the right one is among them.

> *I gathered them all together and I viewed them and I found that a major tribe was missing, a major individual was missing, my life helper was missing, and destiny changer was missing.*

Despite the crowd that was around him, he still had the chance to sit down and ask, "do I have all I need to succeed in this journey?"

In **verse 16** then *I sent for Levi…* Sometimes you need to go the extra mile to send for **what** and **who** you need to make your life or work complete. Folding your hands and hoping that everything will happen by itself will never work. Sometimes you need to get out of your comfort zone to get what you want. But that only comes on a platform of review. There is somebody that God would bring your way to cause the change you need in your life. There is somebody that God will make you have encounter with that will change your level; there is somebody that God will bring in to your destiny that will make you say "wow! I never knew life could be like this."

That person is a **helper of destiny**. That you have a crowd around you may not be sufficient, there is always a need to sit down and review - Do I have the right people, right person, the right individual? Our lives couldn't have been where we are right now without helpers of destiny; God brought a man our way at a point in time who gave us a chance to succeed.

It is not how qualified you are, if you don't have access to that right person at the right time, life will be full of frustrations. That is why once in a while, you just need to sit down and look around and ask, 'do I have all I need to succeed in my life's journey?' Ezra did it and when he found that there was a missing gap, he sent for a Levi, he sent for people to come.

Everybody needs a *Levi* in life. Every believer needs a Levi. You need a Levi irrespective of how knowledgeable you are. The Levi in your life determines how far you go. A Levi could be a man or a woman. A Levi could be your husband or your wife. A Levi could be a colleague or a staff. A Levi could be your driver or your house maid. Don't just assume that everything is in place. Once in a while, sit down and review. Have we done all that we needed to do? Are there things to be done that are not yet done? You need to sit down and begin to review your activities and productivity.

"If you refuse to review you may end up being refused".

If Ezra had assumed that everyone that was relevant or mattered to his destiny were around him, he would have been destroyed. If he assumed that he had all he needed, he would have been destroyed on the way side. It is upon this review that he found out that there was a missing gap.

Every review that does not result in positive changes may not be complete. Reviews trigger changes and reverse the way you operate. For instance, it may be time to build certificates around your skills so that you have enough backing for your capacity. Money isn't everything; learn to review. Get a certificate that will back up your skills and boost your confidence to go anywhere you need to. Enrol into the online universities for your masters; or even Post Graduate Diplomas (PGD). Empower yourself using different e-learning platforms and get a certificate/s.

CHAPTER 47

REVIEW FOR BETTER RESULTS

A life not reviewed, can never be the best. A career not reviewed, may never advance. An organization that does not review what has been done, may live in assumptions that things are working well. It is important as we begin new phases in our lives, to review ourselves, our results, our impacts, our personal growth, and our personal contributions.

The success of any organization is dependent on the success of individual members of the organization. An organization is not the building or the sign post, but the people who make it up. As we move into a new phase, it's important we review for better results.

God reviews, records, and rewards based on his review results. So, why shouldn't we be like Him? As you embark on the process of self and organizational review, ask yourself these questions and document them;

- What are the things I did so well that I'm proud of in the past weeks/months/years?
- What are the things I could have done but didn't do at all that I want to start doing?
- What are the things I did that I should never do again?
- What one thing can I do differently next time?
- What was the best part of my experience this week/month/year?
- What changes would I make if this were my personal business?

Unless you are willing and able to take time out to review and evaluate yourself, one day, when someone external begins to review you, you will get angry. If you have reviewed yourself and identified your weaknesses and strengths, you won't be ignorant when someone else reviews you, identifies your weaknesses/strengths and informs you of them. You'd be able to confidently say '*I know already*' and have begun to work to make the weaknesses better.

In Job 31, Job took out time to review his life and documented his findings. We should do likewise. Stop living in assumptions, stop assuming everything is well, stop assuming everything is right, stop assuming you are the very best at what you do. Step back and review.

Matthew 25:14 "*for the kingdom of heaven is like a man travelling into a far country who called his servants and delivered into his hand goods. To one he gave 5 talents, another two, another one and to everyone according to their several abilities*".

Matthew 25:19 *"the lord of those servants cometh and reckoneth with them after a long time".*

You should keep record of everything. For instance, money you received over the past 5 years and the skills you acquired, what have you done with them? The opportunities that came your way, what did you do with them? The challenges that came, how did you solve them?

If we don't review, we may end up making the same mistakes repeatedly. When we review and identify our errors and mistakes, we will be able to avoid them when moving forward.

Better results are not just a prayer point, they are action points. We must take the required steps to make self-review work. After reviewing, ask yourself questions that will lead to better results like: What can I improve? How can I improve?

There are things that we must continue to do that are good, there are things that we need to drop that are not good, there are things that we need to modify to make them better and there are things we have to start doing that we may not have been doing before. Understanding of these comes from reviews.

4 Fundamental Boosters of Personal Review

1. **Be Honest to yourself:** One wrong you should not do to your destiny is to tell yourself a lie. Someone can come to you and review you but might not know everything about you. You know a lot about yourself.

One serious booster to proper personal review is honesty to yourself. Have I done the best I could have done? Be honest about it. No one is watching you at this point, so choose to be honest to yourself. Am I putting in my very best in what I'm doing? What did I do that I should be doing and what did I do that I should not be doing? Honesty will help you.

2. **Be hard on yourself**: Sometimes we love our comfort zone. If you are not hard on yourself, the world will be hard on you. It's time to say NO to remaining in your comfort zone. Learn to break up your fallow grounds. Everyone has untouched environment, and untapped potential that can be maximized. Break it up! If you normally sleep for too long, shorten it. If you play too much, reduce it. If you spend so much time on Facebook, reduce it. BE HARD ON YOURSELF.

3. **Be willing to change**: For many of us, our biggest enemy in life is our unwillingness to change. To some, it is "As it was in the beginning, so it is now and ever shall it be." You hear people say: *'This is who I am, I can't change, just leave me alone. You either like me as I am or you leave me alone. No big deal'*. You know what is important? Whether you are willing to change or not, you will keep changing. Except you make that conscious decision to change, you would keep changing negatively. Known to you or not, you are changing but your willingness to change will help you positively change your life to the direction you want it to be changed. Be open to corrections from even people who are lower than you, from people who you reverence and who you

do not reverence. The most powerful way to learn is by observation, not instruction, not experience. There is a lot you can change in life by just observing people around you and learning from them.

4. **Ask for grace**: Sometimes, there could be forces around us that could hinder us from being honest to ourselves, from being hard on ourselves and from changing that only grace can deliver. Paul says: "*I am what I am by the grace of God*". That is where the God factor comes in. John 15:5, "*for without me, you can do nothing*". When it gets too tough, just sit down and ask for grace. When it gets difficult, sit down and ask for grace. Why? Because, his grace will always disgrace the enemy trying to make your life miserable.

Be a person that will bring a positive difference. May your impact be felt every day, every week, every month and every year. You will leave a legacy.

CHAPTER 48

PUTTING YOUR MIND TO WORK

1Chronicles 7:40

⁴⁰ All these were the children of Asher, heads of their father's house, choice and mighty men of valour, chief of the princes. And the number throughout the genealogy of them that were apt to the war and to battle was twenty and six thousand men.

Several times we see the Bible refer to people as, "Mighty men of valour". The key phrase is **"mighty men of valour."** One fundamental requirement every man must have to be a mighty man of valour is a **mighty mind**. It takes a mighty mind to be a mighty man. Every mighty man is a man of courage, a man that dares things – a man with a mighty mind!

Your background, qualifications, sex and even colour are completely irrelevant when it comes to this. Who you know is irrelevant. What makes you a man of exploits is a mighty mind. If your mind is feeble, your life remains feeble. Until you have a mind that is at work, no one will mind you. Until you put your mind to work, your life will not matter. Destinies are built by the mind. A mighty mind is a mind of faith, and that makes you dare great things. Friends, you cannot dare great things except your mind can take it. Having a mighty mind is a choice not a gift or a blessing.

Our lives, therefore, are dependent on the state of our minds. The stronger your mind, the mightier your life becomes. Be a mighty man by having a mighty mind. How can you turn your weak mind to a mighty mind?

1. **Guard your mind**: Guard your heart diligently (Proverbs 4:23). What enters your mind feeds your mind, and what feeds your mind shapes your mind. We live in a world where we have free access to all kinds of information which can easily penetrate our minds. If you watch only horror movies, you will have horror dreams; if all you watch is cartoons, pornography, boxing, etc., that is what will fill your mind. Be careful what you listen to and what you watch. It is critical you take control of what is absorbed into your mind. You can choose to block your mind from what you do not like, you can choose to block your mind from what will not make you the great person you desire to be. Guard your mind. As out of the mind proceeds good, bad and all sorts of things. Do not allow anyone corrupt your mind and make it non-functional.

2. **Feed your mind**: Empty minds are dangerous minds. Feed your mind with relevant facts, information, and details. Feed your mind on a regular basis. If you

choose not to feed your mind, the devil will feed it for you free of charge. But if your mind is full, it will be difficult for anyone to put anything into your mind. Stop running around with empty minds. You can feed your mind with God's word (Proverbs 4:20), things that add value to your life, career, profession, ministry and personal interests. Stop going about with empty minds. A very popular proverb says that empty barrel makes the loudest noise. And we all know it is not the noise, but the news that you make that matters.

3. **Rub your mind with great and mighty minds:** Make the right connections, have the right associations, choose the right kind of friends. If you are high up and rub your mind with someone far below, there is high probability you would be dragged downwards. If you do not drink alcohol, and you keep alcoholics as friends, very soon you would join them. Bible says "iron sharpeneth iron" (Proverbs 27:17); and "He that walks with the wise shall be wise, a companion of fools shall be destroyed" (Proverbs 13:20). Rub your mind with great and mighty minds, make the right friends, and always be in the right associations. There are some things you won't learn yourself until someone shows them to you. Learn to learn from others and learn to give to others. We are not created to be alone; that is why God gave Eve to Adam.

4. **Subject your mind to supernatural control**: God is the author of your mind. He knows the plans He has for you. Allow God to guide you, lead you, and govern your mind. He knows your end from the

beginning. Every successful man is someone God has helped. It takes the help of God to be in the right place at the right time for the right opportunity/ opportunities. Allow God to encompass and guide you. I am not a man of myself as I allow God to guide me. Most of the things I do are ordered by God. He has promised to guide and lead you, and the Bible says that they thirsted not when He led them (Isaiah 48:21). When God is leading you, provisions are made available. Do not block your mind away from God's guidance, you will only end up hurting yourself.

In conclusion, please guard your mind against wrong influences, feed your mind with the right things, keep the right company and subject your mind to God's supernatural control. This is the pathway to mighty minds for mighty men.

CHAPTER 49

THE POWER OF CORRECTION

We can learn from anybody and everybody. We can learn even from the less exposed, the so-called illiterate and our subordinates. Learning can take place from every place and every time.

Let's learn from the book of Exodus 18

Exodus 18 VS 13-17

[13] And so it was, on the next day, that Moses sat to judge the people; and the people stood before Moses from morning until evening. [14] So when Moses' father-in-law saw all that he did for the people, he said, "What *is* this thing that you are doing for the people? Why do you alone sit, and all the people stand before you from morning until evening?"[15] And Moses said to his father-in-law, "Because the people come to me to inquire of God. [16] When they have a difficulty, they come to me, and I judge between one and another; and I make known the statutes of God

and His laws."[17] So Moses' father-in-law said to him, *"The thing that you doest is not good.*

I asked my son a few years back *"What is it that Moses did that was not good?"* and he said *"Moses was sitting down and they were standing up all day. Why should he sit down and others stand up? That's unfair."*

Allow me to share with you on the power of correction. "The thing that thou *doest* is not good" Moses was a man that met with God, a man that heard God clearly, a man that had a unique fellowship with God that no one has ever had. And here is a man, a non-Jew, a gentile, telling Moses that what he was doing was not good. Moses could have told the man to keep quiet. How can he understand what he (Moses) was doing? He may even query what Jethro knows about the job. He had every right to castigate Jethro and say you're very stupid, don't tell me what to do. But Moses didn't do any of that; rather, he listened to this man.

The man (Jethro) said (Exodus 18 VS 17-23)..."The thing that you doest *is* not good...you will surely wear yourselves out...select from all the people able men, such as fear God, men of truth, hating covetousness; and place *such* over them *to be* rulers of thousands, rulers of hundreds, rulers of fifties, and rulers of tens...so it will be easier for you, for they will bear *the burden* with you.

And in verse 24 it says; [24] **So Moses heeded the voice of his father-in-law and did all that he had said.**

He (mighty Moses) hearkened unto the voice of his unschooled, unexposed and ungodly father-in-law, and did all he had commanded him. This is Moses, a man of God, the ruler of 3 million plus people. He hearkened unto the voice of a man that has never met God and he did all that the man commanded him.

The Bible later said, Moses was 120 years old and his strength was not abated and his eyes were not dimmed. Do you know why? Because he hearkened to the voice of his father in- law early enough. Every time you hearken to the voice of correction you lengthen your days, maximize your strength, and ensure your well-being. Corrections are ordained from God for our own good. This was not for the good of Jethro, but for Moses. And this became the principle and foundation of three fundamental management principles.

a. **TEAM PRINCIPLE AND LEADERSHIP:** Today we talk about teams; it began from Jethro and Moses. When you hear about teams in management sciences, it is not just a management concept, it is a Biblical concept. Team management began from the Bible. Bible began teams from the very beginning. When you work in Units having a leader, it began from Moses and Jethro. Jethro's advice made him the greatest of all management gurus.

b. **DIVISION OF LABOUR:** When we talk about division of labour, it began from here. Before now, Moses was doing everything himself. Just imagine the Executive Director doing everything in an organization all by himself. He will go to all meetings, write all reports, do all site visits and site preparations, and take all the money alone. Yes, he may become richer, but also, he may never have the time to eat or enjoy the money. That's what Moses was doing here. But Jethro said "You will kill yourself. Give some power/authority to carefully selected people in your group, empower them to do the minor tasks, while you focus on the major assignments. That's what you have in any functional organization. The ED can do all, he has the skills, he has the confidence, but if he does all, he will die. This principle came from Jethro because Moses hearkened to him.

c. **SPECIALIZATION**: When we talk about specialization, it began from Jethro. He emphasized the need for workers and leaders to maximize their strength and focus on where they have strength.

What, therefore, is the power of correction? When we listen to good advice, we become better and do better in life. Moses listened and he became a hero, and lived a less stressful life. When Moses got this work of leading the children of Israel, he sent back his wife and his two sons to his father in Law.

He must have said *"go back to your father, I don't have time for you."* He never asked about them.

It was Jethro who chose to bring them back. He said *"if I allow this man, he will never ask for his wife and children because he doesn't have time for family life".*

But now with appropriate teams, team leadership, division of labour, and specialization, he will have some time for his wife and children.

What am I saying? When you listen to corrections, your burdens are shared and life becomes easy. Don't be an enemy of correction, don't fight anyone that corrects you, gives you instructions and guides you. Anyone that does any of these actually loves you. It is basically not for their benefit, but for yours. My prayer is that you and I will maximize the advantage of correction and become the stars God ordained us to be.

PART 4

BE THE CHANGE

CHAPTER 50

LEAVING A LASTING LEGACY

Living is only meaningful when we leave a legacy. Legacies are not a function of your birth place, your heritage, your qualifications, height, size, complexion, or the amount of money in your bank account. For instance, some people are very wealthy, yet they impact no one. Many have several qualifications, yet ineffective. Legacies can be created by anybody, anywhere, anyhow and in any place. What I am saying is that anyone, educated or not, man or woman, Muslim, Christian or Hindu can leave a lasting legacy.

Globally, there are two kinds of legacies: Good Legacy and Bad Legacy. Both require decisions and choices. I am sure you know people who left good or bad legacies. It is time to be legacy minded. Let me take you back to the Bible and to a Man called Nehemiah:

NEHEMIAH 1:1-3: ... And it came to pass in the month Chisleu, in the twentieth year, as I was in Shushan the palace, ² That Hanani, one of my brethren, came, he and certain men of Judah; and I asked them

concerning the Jews that had escaped, which were left of the captivity, and concerning Jerusalem. ³ And they said unto me, The remnant that are left of the captivity there in the province are in great affliction and reproach: the wall of Jerusalem also is broken down, and the gates thereof are burned with fire.

He was living in the palace and as a cup bearer, he had most things he needed. He was comfortable, well taken care of, and well positioned to enjoy this for life. However, he was worried and sought after the welfare of others. Legacy minded people think about others, ask about others and live for others. When he got the news of the state of his people, he was troubled, cried, fasted and prayed (V4) and then took steps to resolve the issues. And in the sixth Chapter we were told that he solved the problem.

Chapter 6:15 Says; ¹⁵ So the wall was finished in the twenty and fifth day of the month Elul, in fifty and two days.

And because Nehemiah left his comfort zone - the King's palace having identified a problem, took steps despite the threats to his life to solve the problem, today, his name is among the less than 50 people who wrote the 66 books of the Holy Bible.

I am sure that very few of us can easily remember the name of our great grandparents. But names like Albert Einstein, Thomas Edison, Abraham Lincoln, etc. are easily remembered even though they lived and died many years before our great grandparents. Also, men like Isaac Newton, Jesus Christ, Nelson Mandela, etc., are easily remembered. Why? They left behind them notable legacies.

To leave good legacies is a choice, a decision and a product of 5 key things;

1. **Find a problem and solve it**: Legacies are created by problem solvers. If you hate problems, you will never leave a legacy.
2. **Find a challenge and fix it**: Challenges are not enemies of destinies, but pathways to legacies.
3. **Find an issue and resolve it**: Life, company, national or social issues give anybody the needed opportunity to leave a legacy.
4. **Find opportunities and maximize them**: Opportunities abound everywhere. Sometimes they appear in work overalls and do not look like opportunities. Taking a closer look at them, you will find opportunities to explore.
5. **Find people and empower/enable them**: Find individuals who are down in life and empower/ enable them. Legacies are created by individuals who empower and enable others. Nehemiah empowered Israelites even when there was great opposition from Sanballat, Tobiah and others. He gave every worker a gun or a sword and asked them to work, watch and war to protect themselves from the opposition.

To leave a legacy, you must find a problem and solve it, a challenge and fix it, an issue and resolve it, opportunities and exploit them, and people and enable/empower them.

Show me examples of men in the world around us or the Bible who left legacies like Nehemiah, and you have seen men that found issues and resolved them, problems and solved them, challenges and fixed them, opportunities and maximized them, and people who they enabled and empowered. But you must first search and find these problems, challenges, issues, opportunities, and people, before you can solve, fix, resolve, maximize and enable/ empower them respectively.

Friends, the rewards of thinking and leaving legacies are enormous. For instance, Nehemiah was promoted from a house boy position to the governor of an entire country. Why? He did not run from problems, challenges, issues, opportunities and people; rather he went after them and made a name for himself.

If you are not solving problems, fixing challenges, resolving challenges, exploring and exploiting opportunities, and empowering people, you may never leave a legacy. Remember that you do not leave a legacy by the amount of resources you have in your bank account, nor by the number of houses you build, or cars bought. It's about the problems you solved, the challenges you fixed, the issues you resolved, the opportunities you maximized, and the people you empowered. For instance, Prof Herbert Nagasawa, the Scientist behind Riboceine technology, spent 25 years of his life researching because he saw an opportunity, a problem, an issue, a challenge and maximized them. Twenty-four years into the research, people asked him why he was still trying to find this solution. His response was, I am not worried about the number of times I have failed, but I am looking forward to that single time when I will succeed." He succeeded in the 25th year. The world is now enjoying the product of his 25 years of hard work.

In one of the meetings, as I looked at the crowd, I said to myself, life can be interesting when you have a legacy behind you, when people you don't know call your name synonymous to success, e.g., Thomas Edison, Isaac newton, Albert Einstein. We can't live without these people, why? Because they saw a problem and solved them, they saw challenges then fixed them, they saw issues and resolved them, they saw opportunities and explored them; or they found people and empowered them. Don't get carried away by who you think you are or where you think you came from or who you think you are not. The names mentioned above, have fathers, mothers or children who are unknown. It is not a function of your relations, it's a function of your choices and results.

You can come from the wealthiest family in the world or be the daughter of Bill Gates, and add no value and leave no legacy behind. But, you can be a child of the poorest man on earth and yet make a difference. Friends, choose to live a legacy, choose to find a problem and solve it, choose to find a challenge and fix it, choose to find an issue and resolve it, choose to find an opportunity and exploit it, and choose to find people and empower them. That is the pathway to leaving a lasting legacy. Stop looking at your disadvantages, look at your advantages. Stop looking at what you don't have, look at what you have.

A friend told me a few days ago that **"Everything you need to succeed is in you."** So, stop blaming someone for what you don't have. If you don't have what you think you need, then you don't need it now. Everything you need to succeed is in you. You already have them. They are not in anybody's life or anybody's hands, they are in your hands. Begin to look inwards, find the things you have and explore them. Exploring what you have in you is the beginning of making a difference and leaving a legacy.

Be a Nehemiah, David, Joseph, Paul, or Jesus. Leave a lasting legacy for the world.

CHAPTER 51

THE DANGER OF BEING LUKEWARM

Bishop David Abioye said, "those that take life casually die as causalities". He also said that people are low because they are slow. Friends, of all forms of existence, the worst is being **lukewarm**. If you are hot that is good, if you are cold that is also good. But if you are lukewarm, you are a danger to yourself, those around you, and your society.

Revelation 3:14-16

14 And unto the angel of the church of the Laodiceans write; These things saith the Amen, the faithful and true witness, the beginning of the creation of God;15 I know thy works, that thou art neither cold nor hot: I would thou wert cold or hot. 16 So then because thou art lukewarm, and neither cold nor hot, I will spue thee out of my mouth.

The bible says I know thy works. This is encouraging, but also very frightening. People may not know it, but God knows. The truth is that God, Satan and You know exactly who you are! These three personalities are the relevant personalities in your life! Any other person is not so important. If you are not hot and you are pretending to be hot, you are only deceiving yourself. My opinion about you can never change your life. If you are a murderer, and you pretend to be the kindest person on earth then you are deceiving yourself. God knows, Satan knows, you know.

God says in the above scriptures that He knows your works that you are neither hot nor cold. He actually wishes you were either cold or hot so that people can rightly place you where you belong, but because you are lukewarm, He said that He will spit you out of His mouth. This connotes uselessness. When you are brushing your teeth, you spit out the paste, because it is useless after cleaning your mouth. People spit out what is completely useless or dangerous to their health. May God not have a reason to spit you out. May destiny not have a reason to spit you out. May you not be a hindrance to your own greatness in destiny.

Being lukewarm is very dangerous. Going to work is not enough but doing the work is very important. It's either you come to work and do the work or you do not come at all. But that you are occupying the space and being of no relevance is not good. Pretending to work when you are not working is *lukewarm-ness*.

There are many of us whose lives are maimed by lukewarm-ness. They are in church, but not in church. They are home, but not in the home. They are never present even, when they are there. Life is programmed for either hotness or coldness. Lukewarm-ness has no place in destiny. You either agree or disagree in life. You should not be in-between.

Buying of time most times in decision-making is lukewarm-ness, as great and successful men make decisions quickly. It is better to make that decision quickly than stay in a place of immobility because of indecision.

How can you therefore overcome lukewarm-ness?

1. **Build a passion for something**: Let there be something that keeps you awake at night. Develop a passion for something. Let there be something in the next 5 years you would be known for. We live in a world with over 7.6 billion people, do not just be a number – be an individual. Build a passion for something. Steve Jobs said the world is so big, but you can put a dent in the globe. You don't have to change the world, just put a small dent somewhere. Be known for something. Do not stand by the way side gossiping and talking nonsense that will not add value to you. Do not join them in murmuring and complaining all day long. Take steps to change what you do not like. Nigeria is not working, we know. What steps are you taking to make it work? Things are not working, we know. But what steps are you taking to make things work? Life is not where it should be, what steps are you taking to take it there?

2. **Develop a lifestyle of courage**: In life, people can only tell you yes or no. There is no in between. Take

steps. Some men are unmarried because they are afraid to ask a woman to marry them. But, she will either say yes or no. Learn to take off the cloak of lukewarm-ness and take steps with courage. Build the courage to walk towards your passion. Stop being lukewarm. I see the word lukewarm as *looking like worm*. A worm has no spine or bone which connotes lack of courage. It is lack of courage that makes you lukewarm. Build up your courage

3. **Avoid the Nay-Sayers**: Many of us are so conscious of the Nay-Sayers, we never take any meaningful steps in life. Will people tell you no? Yes, they will. It is normal. People will always say "this can't work, this never works", but do not, because of that, be lukewarm. Thomas Edison carried out about 999 experiments before he got the light bulb right. When he was asked what kept him going and why he was so persistent, he said he found 999 ways of doing it wrong. Many of us back out after the 2nd or 3rd failed trial and lose hope. Most times we are just at the 11th hour of our miracles. When you want to break a rock, you hit it many times. It is not the last strike that breaks the rock but a cumulative of all the strikes. Sometimes you must do things again and again and again to get what you want in life. Avoid the Nay-Sayers. When you finally succeed in life, they will come back to you and say things like, "we knew you were going to make it, but...."

Lukewarm-ness makes you look and remain useless. Be hot or be cold. Working is not compulsory, having a job is not compulsory. It's either you are doing the work or not.

There is no in-between. Do not occupy the space doing nothing when someone else can occupy it and do great things. We all are relevant but for your destiny's sake stay where you are most needed and relevant. You do not need to do everything you see. Have passion, have courage, take steps and avoid the Nay-Sayers.

Friends, do not be lukewarm. Rather, anywhere you are found, be relevant. Let someone somewhere remember you for who you are and what you did; and not just your presence. Be remembered for something. Be hot or cold. Do not be lukewarm.

CHAPTER 52

RUN TO WIN

Everybody is in a race. From birth and by divine ordination, we are all in a race. We are either running from something or running towards something, we are either running away from destruction or running into destiny, running to escape or running to obtain.

The moment you are born, the race begins - running from sickness and diseases, or running to prosperity and health; running from joblessness and lack, or running to jobs and profit. We all are in a race.

Some call it the rat race of life, but I call it the divine race. You cannot afford not to be in the race, otherwise your life will have no meaning. At every point in time we are in a race and we should run to win.

However, not everyone who runs wins. In a marathon race, some win, some don't. Likewise, in the race of life, not everyone ends up winning; some win, some lose. Why? Because there are forces fighting against your winning. There are challenges in life you know nothing about which may be hindering you from winning. If you just let your life be the way it is, you will end up not having any say in it. That is why you must run to win.

I want to share a very important principle in winning the race of life. I call this, "the **DEFT Principle**". To be deft means *to be uniquely skilful*, acquiring what is required to succeed. If you do not have a uniqueness in yourself, you will not win the race. Your uniqueness makes you stand out. The components of the DEFT principle are;

1. **Determination**: If you do not determine to do anything, nothing gets done. It takes your primary choice of determination to succeed in the race of life. In order to succeed, you must be determined. Learning from the wise is key to success in life. So, let us look at the wisest man that ever lived in biblical times:

   *And Solomon determined to build a house for the name of the LORD, and a house for his kingdom (*2Chronicles 2:1).

   In order to build the house of God and his own kingdom (run the race to a successful ending), he was determined. Determination to succeed jumpstarts a process that sets things in motion. Moreover, if you do not determine to do something, the devil will determine something else for your life. We are always making decisions. You either make the decision or someone else will make it for you. He decided to build not one but two major houses - for God and Himself.

2. **Engagement:** No matter how good your decision is, if there is no hearty engagement, you will not succeed. Why? Because, for every decision you make, there is a contrary decision that is against it. For instance, if you decide to pass an exam, there is a contrary decision against it; if you decide to have a peaceful home, there is a force against your peaceful home; and if you decide to buy a car, there will be a force against it. Please note that every time you want to do something good, there is a force against it. This is the simple law of life. Thus, to overcome the negative forces against you, you must engage your heart. Even God recognizes those *"that engaged his heart to approach unto me? saith the LORD"* (Jeremiah 30:21).

Without your whole heart in it, success is not attainable as it takes the engagement of the heart to succeed. What does it mean to have your heart engaged? Be courageous, zealous, and passionate about the race. Some of us are so lackadaisical and just watch things happen around us. We say, "Que Sera Sera." There are some habits, attitudes and practices that we must throw into the garbage bag if we must succeed. In your work place, please engage your heart; in your career, marriage, financial destiny, relationships, do well to engage your heart. Things do not just happen, people make things happen.

3. **Focus**: We live in a world of multiple distractions – television, friends, social media, telephone, etc. Every

second something new comes up. Matthew 7:22 says *"...if therefore thine eye be single; thy whole body shall be full of light"*. You cannot go anywhere without focus. If you decide to do something this year; stay focused. If you are determined to marry, build a house, buy a car etc. focus. Focus is the primary force for success.

4. **Timeliness**: Ecclesiastes 3:1 says there is time for everything. If you do not do it at the right time, you might struggle for another 10 years to get it done. Timeliness is one of the greatest friends of successful individuals. I strongly believe in the 10-year cycle for everything. When you miss your time, you may end up spending another 10 years struggling to achieve it. If you miss your turn you might wait for over 10 years to have another chance. Timeliness is everything. Irrespective of how much effort you have put into a task or the amount of resources invested, timeliness can determine success or failure. Remember the ten (10) virgins in the Bible? Timelessness separated the wise from the foolish. You shall not miss your divine appointment!

Apply the DEFT Principle. Be uniquely skilled through determination; heartily engage yourself and your heart in your assigned tasks; focus on your goals and targets; and execute your tasks on time. Remember, everyone is in a race. We are either running from something or running to something, escaping from something or running to obtain, running away from destruction or running towards destiny.

In this race of life, you will win.

CHAPTER 53

FAITHFULNESS BEGETS FRUITFULNESS

Faith is very important. Without it, your being a Christian is of no value. It is the most important aspect of Christianity. Without faith, you cannot receive anything from God. I believe no one comes to God for nothing. The truth is that everyone comes to God for something. Without faith, those things you're coming to God for will not come to you.

Matthew 21:21-22

Jesus answered and said unto them, Verily I say unto you, if ye have faith, and doubt not, ye shall not only do this which is done to the fig tree, but also if ye shall say unto this mountain, Be thou removed, and be thou cast into the sea; it shall be done.[22] And all things, whatsoever ye shall ask in prayer, believing, ye shall receive.

Many times, I have heard people say things like "Forget this prayer thing; all the prayers I have been praying since, what did I get from it?" People start fasting and praying and halfway they get tired and say "all the fasting of last year, what happened, I'm still here". Faithless people easily get tired of waiting, praying or fasting. Some people pray and lose hope before God shows up. It's just an issue of faith.

In the passage above, Jesus is saying, "if you ask, believing in your heart". The Bible also says, if you have faith as a mustard seed, whatsoever you ask, in the name of Jesus will come to pass. It doesn't matter how big it is, even if it's a mountain, it shall be cast out of your way. He saw a fig tree without fruit, just leaves, he cursed it and it withered. The apostles that have been with him all along marvelled. To them, that height of miracle was too extreme. They were wondering how a tree will just wither from its root.

Let us think about how faithful we are. Let us examine our faith. How faithful are we to the Bible we read? Do you believe those things you read there? How much do you believe? Do you believe you can say to sickness be gone and it will go? Do you believe that even with all the ups and downs, you'd still be in abundance? How faithful are you in God that no matter the situation you will get by? Look deep down inside your heart and ask him for the grace to connect with him in faith, we cannot worship him without faith because it is a sin. As whatever is not done in faith is sin.

Looking at it from another dimension

Let us take a while to study the fig tree. Why did God curse the fig tree? He cursed it because it was fruitless. Christ went to that tree very expectant, it was full of leaves, but there were no fruits. He, therefore, cursed the tree and asked it to dry up. If you want to live and make a difference in life and maximize your destiny, one basic requirement is to be fruitful. You have to be full of fruits at all levels; as a husband, wife, staff, parent, church member, community member, you have to bear fruits.

John 15:1 – 2

I am the true vine, and my Father is the husbandman.²Every branch in me that beareth not fruit he taketh away: and every branch that beareth fruit, he purgeth it, that it may bring forth more fruit.

Anywhere you are found at any point in time in life, be fruitful, otherwise you will be a candidate of divine curses. I tell people in my trainings all over the world that if they are downsizing in your organization and you are scared that you will be downsized, then you are not fruitful because nobody will sack his best man. In every aspect of your life, are you fruitful? Because it is your fruitfulness that determines whether you will be cursed or not. Every week, ask yourself "what are the fruits I must bear this week? At your desk; what fruits will I bear?

A Case Study

Let us look at the story of David and Jonathan (2Samuel 9). Jonathan in his lifetime friendship with David bore good fruits. So even when Jonathan and Saul died, David still wanted to bless someone from that family because of Jonathan. They found Mephibosheth who was lame on both legs, and David restored all his father's land to him, gave him a personal servant and he dined at the king's table for the rest of his life. Why? Because of the good fruits one man bore. This is the same David who some days ago, took all the disabled people in the city and killed them, but a lame man had a permanent spot at his dining forever. Why? Because his father bore good fruits.

The good fruit you bear does not end with you, it goes beyond you to your offspring. You do good, not just because of today but because of your posterity. You are doing this, not because of what you will gain now, but what you will gain in the future.

What gives you the capacity to bear good fruit is your faith, as without faith you can't please God. By faith you:

- ➢ Take good steps,
- ➢ Do good things,
- ➢ Bear good fruits,
- ➢ Live a good legacy

PART 5

FACTS OF LIFE

CHAPTER 54

TIMELY WARNING: BEWARE OF ADVISER

Happy New Year and welcome to your year of unquestionable breakthroughs and rewards. You will end this year a surprise to yourself. I am sure you are wondering how - with all the current economic challenges, recession, inflation, new government policies, etc. But I am sure of what I am saying – This shall be a good year, a good year for businesses, marriages, academic excellence, spiritual growth, and even entrepreneurship. Don't you know that light is most beneficial when the darkness is thickest?

Look inwards. Examine yourself. Identify your skills and competences. Be ready to maximize them. This is also a year of misguided representations, bad advice and poor guidance. Thus, I want to share this piece, as it is most appropriate at a time like now. Imagine losing your money to 419 at this time? Imagine not being able to pay your bills because of poor decisions or investments? This is why, you must "beware of advisors".

I am sure you are wondering what gave me the moral audacity to still advise you and call it a warning. Let me take you on a walk.

December 26, 2016 was a great day. I hosted a lot of people from all over the world – USA, Italy, Cameroon, Nigeria, etc. It was a great gathering indeed! Many also came from my village, town and neighbouring cities. Since a very big cow laid down its life for the occasion, enemies and friends alike gathered; some to celebrate, the rest to eat of the abundance of God's gifts. It was a great outing. The objective was met. However, everyone had his or her baggage. People talked to me on several issues. Some complained about neglect and maltreatment. While some gave me advise on several personal and family issues. I also heard from some people who were giving lectures on a number of current and topical problems facing the community and the nation.

My question is, who is advising you? The person speaking to you about marriage, does he/her have a good marriage? The person spending time advising you on how to manage mothers-in-law, does she have one? The one advising you on how to be a good wife or husband, what are the testimonies of their husband/wife about them? The ones speaking to you on finances, health, spirituality, or even relationship, are their finances, health, spirituality or relationship healthy and enviable?

Beware of unsolicited advice. Many unsolicited advisers speak to you from the abundance of their hearts – what they have is what they can give. And nobody can ever give what he or she does not have. For instance, you cannot give advice on how to live peaceably with all men when you are quarrelsome with many. You cannot advice on how to be wealthy, when you cannot pay your personal bills. You cannot advice on how to manage a business, when many businesses have failed in your hands.

It is what a man has that he gives. When I finished medical school, I had a number of lecturers who advised me on what next to do. I looked at them, and did not like what I saw. I did not want to end my life like them. To me, although they were doing well as lecturers and professors, I did not want to be like them. So, I rejected their pieces of advice. I chose my own path in life. Today, I celebrate that decision and I am proud to be where I am – doing what I love most – preventing diseases and giving hope and health to the sick.

The recent pieces of advice in my village were similar – from people who I do not envy or desire to ever be like. The married ones had troubled homes; and although they may not know it, they are part of their troubles. Thus, their advice (if accepted and implemented) may end up resulting in troubles in my family. For instance, how can somebody who despises his or her spouse help you to love your spouse?

Beware of pieces of advice coming from the wrong quarters. Stay clear of people who waste your time talking to you about people you know, love or are related to. Beware of people who waste time telling you of things you never knew about others to discredit them. Beware of people who can spend the entire day talking about others. Remember, people who talk about others to you, will talk about you to others.

CHAPTER 55

4 FUNDAMENTAL RESPONSIBILITIES OF LEADERSHIP

Every leader has several responsibilities to him/herself, followers, organization, and society. These are critical to the success of the leader both as an individual and as a leader. Every responsible organization is a platform for the development of leaders. No staff should remain a follower for life. Anyone could start as a follower, but must *choose to be a leader.* Any contrary choice is a choice made against your destiny. Do not remain a child forever – otherwise you will miss life opportunities and great rewards. Hear what Galatians 4:1 says;

Now I say that the heir, as long as he is a child, does not differ at all from a slave, though he is master of all,

My sincere prayer is that none shall die a child, a follower or a nonentity. What are therefore these four fundamental responsibilities of leadership?

1 Samuel 12:23-24

[23] *Moreover as for me, God forbid that I should sin against the LORD in ceasing to pray for you: but I will teach you the good and the right way:* [24] *only fear the LORD, and serve him in truth with all your heart: for consider how great things he hath done for you.*

From the above scripture;

1. **Leaders pray for their followers**: Actually, it is a sin not to pray for your followers. It is a sin against God and humanity if, as a supervisor, team leader, manager or executive officer, you do not make out time to pray for that person(s) you are supervising, leading, or managing. Anybody under your supervision - be it your wife, child(ren), house-help, church member, work colleague – should benefit from your prayers. It is a sin if you do not pray for them. This is why Jesus took a whole chapter of John to pray for both his current and future followers (John 17). Not praying for your subordinates may result in avoidable challenges and issues that could have been handled on the altar of prayer. As a leader, pray for the perceived and actual personal needs of all your followers at least once every week. When the bible says be your brother's keeper, it is not only about guidance and counselling, although these are very important; but it talks also about spiritual health. Each of us has a divine responsibility that goes beyond sharing things to praying for one another.

The bible says it is a sin if leaders fail to pray for their followers. When last did you pray for someone in your office, someone that works with you, or is under your supervision? Stop complaining about the person not doing well. It is time to start praying for them because so many issues can be resolved on the altar of prayer. Believers of today have a habit of saying, "Lord give me, give me, give me". They do this Monday through Sunday. Every request they make is just about themselves. Friends, stop being selfish. The Bible says *"and the Lord turned around the captivity of Job when he Prayed for his friends"* (Job 42:10). When last did you mention someone's issue in your private prayers? If I look at your prayer request, how many of them are about someone else? Lord, I want this, I want that. The Lord is asking; when will you grow up? I adjure you to change your mentality from being self-centred to being people oriented. Think on this and improve your ways.

2. **Leaders are teachers**: *"But I will teach you the good and the right way...."* Leaders teach – they teach joyfully and willingly. They are always glad to share knowledge with people and empower people to succeed. If you have kept what you know to yourself, and have never shared with someone else, then you are not a leader. Leaders are teachers. They do not teach the bad way, they teach the right way. The essence of leadership is to pull people from where they are to where they ought to be. The essence of leadership is to make people better than

what they are. If you stay in any organization for one year and your life does not change, then something is wrong with your leaders or you!

Samuel said "*I will teach you the good and the right way*". Why? Because the biggest room in the world today is the room of improvement, no matter how much you know today, there is a lot more you do not know yet. I have a DrPH (Doctor of Public Health), which can be seen as the highest level of academic knowledge, but there are still a lot I don't know. Life is all about continuous, lifelong learning. It is not just about the degree, but the insight. Leaders who do not develop themselves, deliver obsolete knowledge to their followers, and this can easily put them in trouble. Leaders should teach the good and the right way. Those who think they will lose relevance by sharing what they have, end up becoming nonentities in the journey of life. Teach to make yourself a better person!

3. **Leaders respect authority**: *Verse 24 says "only fear the Lord."* Leaders respect constituted authorities. Authority that you do not respect cannot profit/help you. If you have the kind of mentality that makes you better than your supervisors, you will have major issues. You will never learn from people you do not respect and reverence. There is always someone above you. Every leader, supervisor, CEO, board, and president has someone above him/her. Every good leader respects authority. This ignites followers respect automatically. The concept of "do you know

who I am?", "why are you talking to me like that?" is a failed concept. We all need each other to succeed and survive. Leaders respect authority, It doesn't matter whether the person is older or younger than you, leaders respect authority. Romans 13:1 says; *Let everyone be subject to the governing authorities, for there is no authority except that which God has established. The authorities that exist have been established by God.*

If God puts someone who is younger than you above you, it may be to test your humility, meekness and willingness to learn. But some people have denied themselves the access to learn because of who they think they are. But who are you? If you sleep and do not wake, that is the end. Friends, leaders respect authority.

4. **Leaders provide services**: Leadership is not just about giving instructions; it is primarily about serving. Jesus said *"I am among you as one that serves"* (Luke 22:27). It is not about folding your arms and issuing instructions. Leaders provide service(s). When the going gets tough, leaders take over. When the work seems impossible, leaders make it cheaply possible. Leaders are known by the services they provide. And, if you fail to serve, you may never lead. Leaders offer services to their organizations, subordinates, customers, and even servants. They serve those that are following them. Like Jesus, you should wash the legs of those following you. You

should nurture them, care for them; and provide relevant services to them.

Remember, **leadership is not a title, it is a responsibility.** Leadership is not about who you are, it is about what responsibility(ies) you are willing to carry. As a wife, husband, staff, worker, etc., in the position of leadership, you are required to;

1. Pray ceaselessly for your followers,
2. Teach your followers the right and good way;
3. Respect authority; and
4. Serve others.

CHAPTER 56

WHO IS YOUR FRIEND?

Let me ask you a very vital question; Who is your friend? Why? It's because life and destiny are determined and shaped/sharpened by friendship. Who is your friend? Let us take our scriptural reading from Judges 9:4

⁴ And they gave him threescore and ten pieces of silver out of the house of Baalberith, wherewith Abimelech hired vain and light persons, which followed him.

Who is your friend? Are they vain and light persons? Are they individuals who will help you focus on a vision and achieve it, or those that will help in destroying you, your vision and future? Who is your friend? As men and women who want to marry, who are in school, or even in a workplace, ask yourself again now; who is your friend?

Lives have been destroyed by friendship. Also, destinies have been moulded by friendship. People have moved forward in life through friends, people have also been broken by friends. Who is your friend?

In Igbo they say *"I gosi m ndi enyi gi, aga m agwa gi onye I bu"* meaning show me your friend and I will tell you who you are. If your friends are thieves, drunkards, liars, drug addicts; even if you are not one now, sooner or later, you will join them! Who is your friend? This is a question that determines if you will live or die. If you read the latter part of same chapter (Judges 9), Abimelech was killed. In one chapter, he rose up, made friends of vain and light fellows, and by the end of the chapter, he was killed by a woman.

Everyone has a glorious destiny, but the people you surround yourself with will determine how far you will go. Who is your friend? Are you proud of the people you associate with or do you only meet with them at night? If you have friends that you meet only at night, then you're in a wrong association. If you hide your friends and save their name in your phones with codes, if you have to hide their identity because you're not proud of them, then you're on the wrong track.

In the Bible, the friendship of Jonathan and David added values to their lives. But that of Amnon and Jonadab resulted in the destruction of Amnon. Be careful of who you choose as friends. Choose to actively deliver yourself from wrong friendships and associations. Verse 5 says;

5 And he went unto his father's house at Ophrah, and slew his brethren the sons of Jerubbaal, being threescore and ten persons, upon one stone: notwithstanding yet Jotham the youngest son of Jerubbaal was left; for he hid himself.

You must deliberately choose to hide yourself from wrong people and wrong influence if you must secure your life and destiny. There are some things you should consciously abstain from. For instance, that you have 24/7 internet does not mean you should be careless. Hide yourself from certain things if you want to live a healthy life. The ability to hide oneself or abstain from some things is not a function of age, or exposure. Gideon's sons were men of war, but were slaughtered on one stone by Abimelech and his vain and light friends. Only Jotham, the youngest and inexperienced, who hid himself, survived. Take deliberate steps to cover and hide yourselves from destruction.

CHAPTER 57

THE POWER OF CHOICE

Choice is everything. We choose what to wear, where to go, what course to read, what career to pursue, who to marry, what or who to worship, which programs to attend, what to eat, where to live, and even when to play, enjoy, eat or sleep. The choices we make in life affects everything that we do.

Joshua said.

"And if it seems evil to you to serve the LORD, choose for yourselves this day whom you will serve, whether the gods which your fathers served that were on the other side of the River, or the gods of the Amorites, in whose land you dwell. But as for me and my house, we will serve the LORD."(Joshua 24:15).

The above scripture is so interesting. Just imagine somebody telling you right now, "Choose you this day whom you will serve, choose you this day what you will do with your life, choose you this day what your legacy would be, etc." I know you have heard enough sermons in church on this subject, which is why I shall be taking it from a different dimension in this chapter.

Today, the offer is open unto you. Choose you this day what you will do with your time, life, family, friends, finances, intellect, certificate, food, strength, and energy. Everything about life is premised on this word **CHOICE**. Your clothing this morning was your choice. The ties, shirts, and underwear you are dressed in right now were your choice. The shoes you are wearing, your hair style, your make-up, are all based on choice.

Actually, in life there are very few things you can't choose. For instance, you cannot choose your parents, and you cannot choose when and where to be born. But beyond these, you have a choice to make in almost all things. You can even choose when to die and how to die. People today choose when to die, how to die, and where to die. Friends, they choose! People choose where to be buried, how to be buried, how much should be spent, etc. People choose who to live with and who not to live with. Everything about life is premised on the word choice.

"Choose you this day whom you will serve". In other words, choose you this day how your life will go, the way of your parents or the way you have decided? Choose you this day how you will end your career, the way your parents ended theirs or the way you have chosen to end it. Friends choose you today who you will marry. Choose ye who you will love, choose ye who you will work with. Choose, friends, choose.

Choose ye whether you want to be a parasite, symbiotic or a commensal in relationships - whether you want to add value or subtract value. Choose ye this day what legacy you will leave. In forty years from now, what legacy will they remember you for? Choose you this day what your life will be at fifty. Choose you this day how long you will pay house rent. Choose you this day how long people will laugh at you, or celebrate you. Everything about life is premised on the word choice.

Choose you this day what you want the next ten years, twenty, thirty, forty years to be like. Let me will share with you four fundamental requirements for good choice.

FOUR FUNDAMENTAL REQUIREMENTS FOR GOOD CHOICE:

1. ***Understand where you are going***: What you want out of life is your choice, what you want out of your marriage is also your choice. If you want intelligent children, marry an intelligent spouse, there is no need getting married to a dull spouse and asking God for intelligent children. For you to make the right choice, you must know where you are going to in life. It is not where you are now that is important, it is where you are going to, and that is the most important issue. If you do not know where you are going, every choice will be the right one. Understand where you are going to and focus on it.

2. ***Understand the requirements for your choice***: Every choice has a price that must be paid. For instance, if you want to stop paying house rent, there is a price to pay. If you want to stop alcoholism, there is a price. For some people, the amount of money spent on alcohol in 10 years can build a

house. Understand the price and requirement for your choice.

3. ***Understand the prize for not making a good choice***: In economics, there is what we call "opportunity cost". For every choice you make or do not make, there is a prize in it. Assess yourself, your capacity to execute the choice. Several times, we make choices and forget to look at our strengths and weaknesses. It occurred to me that everybody has a demon they are dealing with. No matter how much you want to be perfect, there is always a force that is trying to hold you back from making the right choices. Therefore, look at yourself, look at your potentials; how can you maximize yourself to get what you want out of life? Ask yourself this question, what will it take to get to where I want to be in life? It is only when you have assessed yourself and you have been able to identify your strengths and the weaknesses that is when your choices will not be frustrated. Many a times our choices turn out to be frustrations to us, because we have not had time to assess ourselves and know our weaknesses and strength.

4. ***Assess your capacity to execute the right choice***: There are some choices you cannot make in life and you will not be able to identify those choices if you do not assess yourself accurately. Look for those who have the results you desire. You must know the price to pay for the choice you make, you must also know the price for not making the choice, and you should also have a sense of direction, and also know what it takes to make the right choices.

CHAPTER 58

YOU HAVE ALL IT TAKES

Judges 6:15-16.

¹⁵ And he said unto him, Oh my Lord, wherewith shall I save Israel? Behold, my family is poor in Manasseh, and I am the least in my father's house.¹⁶ And the LORD said unto him, surely I will be with thee, and thou shalt smite the Midianites as one man.

Gideon had all the good excuses. Hear him, "My family is amongst the poorest and I am the least in my father's house. How can I make a difference? My father has no identity and I have the worst identity myself. How can I live a life of impact when I do not have the qualification in terms of size or academic qualification, how can I make a difference when I do not have the right connections in life?"

You have all it takes to make a difference and leave a legacy. You have all it takes to be a multi-billionaire, to achieve your visions, and become whatever you want to be in life. Your family lineage is irrelevant; your position in the family is immaterial. Why? Because you have all it takes. Look at the stories of great men today; you will be amazed to know of their humble background. Most world-renowned men have no special family background, parental upbringing, and silver spoon background.

Great men and women are people who chose to take their destinies in their hands and run with it, and today they have become global phenomenon. We have all it takes. In the passage above, Gideon said, *"my family is the least in Benjamin, my family is the least in Manasseh."* In other words, I am not qualified because my family is not qualified, my family is poor, my family is unknown, my family had never led before, my family has no voice, etc. Are you thinking and talking like Gideon? Are you seeing yourself as a grasshopper before your life challenges?

Because of his thought process, a mighty man of valour was hiding from the Midianites, threshing wheat (*12 And the angel of the LORD appeared unto him, and said unto him, The LORD is with thee, thou mighty man of valour.)*

God did not come down and put mightiness into him or put a mighty strength upon him, No! It was already inside him, but he never knew it. He was hiding from the Midianites, despite all the potentials that God put in him. It is because he saw himself in a wrong light. Are you suffering from **Gideon's syndrome?**

How do you see yourself? Have you ever for once sat down to appreciate God for who you are? God did not make a mistake in creating you and equipping you to be who you are. God kept you so you can make a difference, so that you may leave a legacy. You have all it takes to be the very best of what you want to be, you have all it takes to be a voice for your family, you have all it takes to be the saviour of your nation. Yes, you have all it takes!!!

What is the difference between you and your leaders for instance? Or between you and the former President of your country? What is the difference? In truth, you may have more than they have. Just understand that you have all it takes. Stop looking down on yourself, stop promoting a negative narrative of yourself, stop seeing yourself through the eyes of a grasshopper. Many of us belittle ourselves so much that we fail to deliver the kind of results that we ought to deliver, because we have seen ourselves as "never do well", people have called you all manner of names in school and in life, and so you began to run your life by those names.

In the '80s, when I was writing my WASC (this is the Secondary School Certificate Examination), one of my teachers came into my exam hall and whipped me. He whipped me because my pencil was short. He called me a dunce, a never do well, and prophesized that I will never pass the exams. As a young boy, I cried in that exam hall. However, when the result came out, I was the best student in the whole school. And, on the day I went to collect my result, he was in the principal's office. He stood up to congratulate me. Maybe he even forgot what he said, but I did not. Rather than allow what he said deter me, it spurred me unto greater heights.

Do not accept the labelling of men, do not belittle yourself. I stammered so badly that I sometimes had to hit my feet on the floor to communicate. But I refused to accept that label. I used to have very big pimples on my face and was called pimple orchard. That was enough to make me have low self-esteem – but it did not. I did not allow it. Do not allow your present condition to determine your future destination. Do not belittle yourself or let any man belittle you. Any labelling you reject may actually position you for greater exploits in life.

Beginning from now, see yourselves from the light of the scriptures. There is much more in you that you could ever imagine. Gideon thought God was joking, but with 360 men, he fought and defeated the Midianites.

There is so much more in you, intellectually, economically, spiritually, relationship wise - there is much more in you. Do not allow anybody living or dead to make you feel inferior, you are not inferior to anybody. Somebody may be up there today who has a house or a car; friends, you are not inferior because you are on your way, in a short while you will take over, and then you will have a voice in your environment.

Make up your mind for a quantum leap across all aspects of life, You must first believe in yourself. You must then understand who you are, and agree with God that with him all things are possible. Judges 6:16 says,

16 And the LORD said unto him, Surely, I will be with thee, and thou shalt smite the Midianites as one man.

You do not need a crowd to make a difference. Understand that if any man can succeed, you too can succeed; if any man can make a difference, you can make a difference; and if any man can become wealthy in life, you can become wealthy in life.

This year is an opportunity you cannot afford to miss. There is an opportunity for unusual progression in every area of life. Begin to package and repackage yourself right now before the end of the year. Do not wait for the 31st of December to start making New Year resolutions. Start now to package yourself and position yourself for what you want to see in the coming years.

CHAPTER 59

MAXIMIZING THE FOUR DIMENSIONAL PERSONALITY OF GOD

I know you must have been told that we serve a merciful God. But, we serve a God who has four critical dimensions. Sometimes we think we now know and understand God until He reveals another side of Himself to us. We should maximize the Four-Dimensional Personality of God – but this can only happen when we understand these dimensions.

Somebody maybe saying – But God is the same yesterday, today and forever (Hebrew 13:8). Yes, you are right. But the unchangeable changer of destinies has four sides to His personality. I am not talking about the trinity, but a God that could be four different things based on how we relate to Him and what we do.

The Bible said, *"¹⁷And there shall cleave nought of the cursed thing to thine hand: that the Lord may turn from the fierceness of his **anger**, and shew thee **mercy**, and have*

compassion *upon thee, and* **multiply** *thee, as he hath sworn unto thy fathers."*(Deuteronomy 13:17).

We serve a God who could be angry, merciful, compassionate and also multiplicative. Let me take you on a simple journey today.

1. **The Angry God:** We serve a God who can be angry. Psalm 7:11 said...*God is angry with the wicked every day.* In Genesis, Adam and Eve disobeyed God and ate the forbidden fruit. The angry God pronounced a curse on them, on the serpent and on the land for their sake. Cain misbehaved by killing his brother Abel, so God cursed him. Moses married from the "wrong" tribe – an Ethiopian woman. This was completely against the commandments of God. Mariam and Aaron stood in judgment and spoke against him. Moses didn't hear them, but God heard from heaven. The Lord was angry, spoke suddenly and placed a curse on Mariam and Aaron and Mariam became leprous (Number 12:1-10). In Numbers 16 when Korah, Dathan, and Abiram spoke against Moses, the angry God descended and "the earth opened her mouth, and swallowed them up, and their houses, and all the men that appertained unto Korah, and all their goods." (Vs 32). These are the manifestations of an angry God!

    Several times, people forget this side of God – the angry God. God is angry with the wicked every day! He killeth and maketh alive, He healeth and woundeth. God's children are also permitted to be angry. But hear God, ...*Be ye angry, and sin not: let not the sun go down upon your wrath (Ephesians 4:26).* Even Jesus took a cane and began to flog both men and women buying and selling in the temple, saying... *It is written, My house shall be called the house of prayer; but ye have made it a den of thieves (Matthew 21:13).* So being angry does not make you ungodly unless you are angry for the wrong reasons.

Currently, many people are suffering and struggling under the bondage of divine anger but there is good news for you this morning, we serve....

2. **A Merciful God**: ...*and showed thee* **mercy**. God is also a merciful God. In Lamentation 3:12 ...*It is of the Lord's mercies that we are not consumed, because His compassions fail not.* It is His mercy that saved us. His mercy redeemed us such that while we were yet sinners, Christ died for us. His mercy turns our mess into messages and miracles. His mercy covers our errors and colours our efforts. His mercy is what has wiped away our shame and given us a new song to sing.

Peradventure you are currently suffering because of His anger, His mercy is available to you. His mercy will wash us and make us purer than gold. Our merciful God is also...

3. **A Compassionate God**: ....*and have* **compassion** *upon thee.* Our God normally has compressed passion concerning our affairs. Psalms 8:4 and

115:12 says that God is so mindful of you and me. No matter what you are going through in life, don't think that God does not know. God knows. He is mindful of you and me. Yes, we live in a country where everything is becoming so tough; but He says; "At destruction and famine thou shalt laugh" (Job 5:22). Though everything may become so expensive and salary does not change, stand on his promises – in famine, you shall laugh!

Understand that when you are going through trials, God is there with and for you. There is nothing that you are passing through right now that your heavenly Father does not know. Do not carry that burden alone, share it with God, He is compassionate and ready to help you. He says, *Come unto me, all ye that labour and are heavy laden, and I will give you rest...(Matthew 11:28).* Allow Him to help you. But He can't give you rest until you come, and coming to Him is a personal decision.

If you refuse to cast your burden on Him then He will leave you alone; but if you come and lay it at His feet, then He will give you rest because living on God's compassion is the easiest way to live. Remember, labouring without God can lead to your destruction. Psalms 127:1 says *Except the Lord build the house, they labour in vain that build it: except the Lord keep the city, the watchman waketh but in vain. 2 It is vain for you to rise up early, to sit up late, to eat the bread of sorrows: for so he giveth his beloved sleep.*

4. **The Multiplying God:**...*and multiply thee.* God multiplies His blessings upon His children. In Genesis 1:28, He commanded, *"Be fruitful and multiply....* He has unlimited capacity to multiply you. Deuteronomy 1:11says *The Lord God of your fathers make you a thousand times so many more as ye are, and bless you, as he hath promised you!* God will multiply His blessings in your life, family, marriage, career, business, and finances. The barren will conceive and bring forth twins and triplets, the jobless shall have jobs and become employers of labour, the singles shall be married and become joyful mothers of children, the homeless shall become owners of houses and landlords, where you were despised, God shall make you an eternal excellency. His multiplying grace shall work for you.

However, how can you access God's multiplication, mercy and compassion and avoid His anger? Hear from the same Chapter:

6 *If thy brother, the son of thy mother, or thy son, or thy daughter, or the wife of thy bosom, or thy friend, which is as thine own soul, entice thee secretly, saying, Let us go and serve other gods, which thou hast not known, thou, nor thy fathers;*

To enjoy the best of God say no to what is wrong and yes to what is right. Never allow anything or anybody – including people who are so close to you – to derail your destiny.

The Bible commands, *"Thou shalt not **consent** unto him, nor **hearken** unto him; neither shall thine eye pity him, neither shalt thou spare, neither shalt thou conceal him: But thou shalt surely **kill** him…And thou shalt **stone** him with stones…"* (V8-10).

A word is enough for the wise!! Be and remain blessed.

CHAPTER 60

FIT OR MISFIT

In life, you are either a "fit" or a "misfit". Actually, once you are not a 'fit", you are a "misfit". Today, many are misfits without even knowing it. Are you a "fit" or a "misfit"?

In Acts Chapter 1:16–23, we saw the Apostles trying to replace one of them who messed up and died a stupid death – Judas. He was a typical round peg in a square hole! To replace him, Peter had to make sure that they did not make another mistake, so he defined the qualifications of the right "fit"

Act 1: 16

21 Wherefore of these men which have companied with us all the time that the Lord Jesus went in and out among us, 22 Beginning from the baptism of John, unto that same day that he was taken up from us, must one be ordained to be a witness with us of his resurrection. 23 And they appointed two, Joseph called Barsabas, who was surnamed Justus, and Matthias.

From about 120 persons in the room, only two qualified to be nominated. You may be beautiful or handsome, educated or even super-educated, well connected or not, but the question this morning is, "Are you a fit or a misfit?" Do you properly fit into your role? - Are you a square peg in a square hole or a round peg in a square hole? In your relationship(s), family, among your friends, church, or even in your place of work - are you a fit or a misfit?.

In life, there are two types of problems: technical problems and adaptive problems. While technical problems are responsible for about 5% of all life problems, adaptive problems account for the remaining 95% of problems faced by people. Technical problems require skills and expertise to be resolved, such as failed engines, computer, etc. Adaptive problems require personal efforts and decisions to resolve them – such as sleeping habit, eating habits, etc. To be a "fit" or a "misfit" is not a function of colour, race, complexion, height or qualification. It is just a function of adaptive behaviour!

You may be the most qualified person but unfit in the system; you may even be the richest man or woman, but unfit. The ability to fit in is never a function of colour, size, religion, or tribe. It is primarily a function of adaptability. To be fit, you may have to "panel beat" your character, attitude, behaviour or even tongue. Change is a choice! You have the freedom to take any step, make any choice or decision, but you do not have the freedom to determine the consequences! Even not deciding to decide is a choice.

Anybody can change and it may require you to go the extra mile, but it is always worth it. Whatever you want in life you can get by effective "panel beating" of your self – you may have to panel beat your behaviour, attitude, friends, associates, etc. to get to where you want to get to in life.

You truly do not need some baggage you are carrying. Nobody ever runs 100m race in trousers or plays football in a three-piece suit. Wearing the wrong outfit will always make you appear stupid. In the race of life, there are some baggage you don't need. Avoid them!

Everything about life is a product of choices. You work in an organization by choice. Your dress, your hair style, your shoes, your breakfast (if you have had one), etc. are all products of choices you made. Make an additional choice to off load every baggage.

In life you can either be a fit or a misfit. What looks good on someone else may not look good on you. Judas would have had a glorious destiny but he was a "misfit", and to replace him only two out of one hundred and twenty people met the criteria. Are you the right specification for the task God has assigned? That you are present does not mean you are a fit. In your office, in your career, in your relationship, in your marriage; choose to be a fit! Make a choice this morning to fit into the system, into your role, and into the group. As a lady, man, father, mother or a staff, choose to be a fit. As a single young lady choose to be a fit so that men can propose to you; as a mature bachelor, choose to be a fit so that women can agree to marry you.

Whatever baggage you are carrying now that would cause you not to be a fit; drop them! It could be your friends, your contacts, social media, movies, football, or unnecessary visitations.

CHAPTER 61

ACCESSING YOUR WEALTHY PLACE

Psalm 66:12: *"Thou hast caused men to ride over our heads; we went through fire and through water: but thou broughtest us out into a wealthy place."*

Thou hast caused men to ride over our heads. Friends! Not every challenge is caused by devil. God allows some life challenges. Not every problem is designed to destroy you; some of them are designed to make you a better person. Not every problem is a disaster, because problems are part of our lives; nobody enjoys passing through fire, it is never a comfortable experience.

Even though we celebrate Shadrach, Meshach and Abednego who were able to pass through fire with God (the fourth man amidst them), I am so sure that it wasn't a great experience. Daniel stayed in the lions' den for a whole night. Even though God was there to shut the lions' mouths, yet staying in the lions' den can never be a nice experience. Paul and Silas were in prison and they worshipped and praised God. Even though God delivered them, staying in a prison is an experience most people would rather not have.

Friends, there are things you may be passing through right now that may not be pleasant. The truth is this, everybody passes through something at some periods of their lives, and I mean everybody. David Oyedepo, Enoch Adeboye, Chris Oyakilome, Pastor Kumuyi, Obinna Oleribe, yourself, everybody at any point in time is passing through something.

...we went through fire and through water....;

But why should God allow you to pass through fire and water at the first instance? To everyone there is a wealthy place; to every destiny there is a wealthy place; to every family there is a wealthy place; to every life, there is a wealthy place. But, you can't access the wealthy place until you have passed through fire and water, you cannot access the wealthy place until you have passed through certain life challenges successfully. Why? Because gold is not very useful until it has passed through fire. The quality of gold is a function of the intensity and duration of exposure to fire. The hotter the fire the purer the gold. ***God allows you and I to pass through the fire because He wants to make us better, purer, move valuable and more productive.*** He wants to make us become holier, stronger and more refined. Do you not remember that nobody can ever become a graduate without passing through school? You cannot become a physician without passing your examinations. When God sees your effort in passing through, He brings you to your wealthy place.

Please also note that your zeal and passion alone cannot get you into your wealthy place; it takes God to bring you from where you are to your wealthy place. Wealth here means wealth of joy, wealth of favour, wealth of happiness, wealth of fulfilments, wealth of career excellence, wealth of marital dignity, etc. Wealthy place! It takes God to bring you there, but He will not bring you until you have shown your faithfulness amidst your current challenges. You are passing through something now, it's not the end. Women forget their pains of labour after they deliver the baby.

The good news is that before He made you, He created your wealthy place. However, it will take your willingness to pass through to partake in it.

How do we get to the wealthy place?

Psalm 19:11, 14: *Moreover by them is thy servant warned: and in keeping of them there is great reward. Let the words of my mouth, and the meditation of my heart, be acceptable in thy sight, O LORD, my strength, and my redeemer.*

The words of your mouth create your destiny therefore be mindful of what you say, be mindful of what you pronounce *"as a man thinketh in his heart so is he" (Proverbs 23:7).*

Remember, your thoughts become your words, your words become your actions, your actions become your character, your character becomes your habits, and your habits define your destiny. Whoever you are today is the product of your thoughts yesterday. Think well, think wealthy, think success, think victory, and think impact. Open up yourself for a while and stop being too selfish, stop being too self-centred. What will you be remembered for after you are no more? Think legacy and leave a legacy.

Finally, hear God: "*Having therefore these promises, dearly beloved, let us cleanse ourselves from all filthiness of the flesh and spirit, perfecting holiness in the fear of God*". **2Corinthians 7:1**.

Get ready for your wealthy place.

CHAPTER 62

GOD IS STILL AT WORK

You may be going through stuff; I understand and do care. You may be carrying a heavy burden right now, too difficult to handle alone; I also understand and can identify with you. People may have said all manner of negative things about you, and you are just confused and wondering what next to do. Just understand that **God is still at work**.

Like Zechariah, there could be horns against your destiny and future.

Zechariah 1:18 - 19

¹⁸Then lifted I up mine eyes, and saw, and behold four horns. ¹⁹And I said unto the angel that talked with me, What be these? And he answered me, These are the horns which have scattered Judah, Israel, and Jerusalem.

You may be seeing the horns right now. You may have seen pain, shame, reproach, mockery, diseases, barrenness, infertility, losses, etc. Yes, you may have seen it all. You may have seen the horns that scattered your destiny, the challenges that made your live unattractive, the problems that made you think your case is the worst in the whole world. There are various horns of the devil that have scattered people's destinies, marriages, careers, finances, families, ministries, health, etc.

Take a look at the verse again. These horns did terrible things to **Judah, Israel, and Jerusalem**. These are three cities that belong to God – The Almighty God, Jehovah Over-do. They are towns and cities dear to God – the all-powerful God, managed by God, protected and provided for by God, and yet they were scattered by the horns of the wicked one.

Somebody may be asking, why me? Why am I going through all these, even though I serve God and, maybe, pay my tithe? You are a Judah, an Israel, and a Jerusalem!

Someone else is asking, why should God be watching with His angels, as Satan and his demons scatter God's own cities and towns, His own people and nations, His own children and apples of His eyes? Why?

Just listen for a moment. God has a word for you. He is showing you something right now…are you seeing?

He is showing you four Carpenters (*20And the Lord shewed me four carpenters.*).

I am sure, you are confused. Not to worry. You are not the first. Hear this…

²¹ *Then said I, What come these to do? And he spake, saying, These are the horns which have scattered Judah, so that no man did lift up his head: but these are come to fray them, to cast out the horns of the Gentiles, which lifted up their horn over the land of Judah to scatter it.*

There is good news right now – God has FOUR Carpenters!!!! For every horn scattering, there is a divine carpenter; for every devastation of Satan, there is a divine solution. For every horn, there is a carpenter to rebuild and restore. They are mandated by God to work out your restoration, and to deliver the long-awaited change in your life.

Friends, God is still at work, God cannot just see you amidst challenges and keep quiet. He has sent His carpenters. God is faithful. God is awesome!

Understand that what was scattered was Jerusalem, Israel, and Judah; not the Amorites, Moabites, or other gentile! If you are going through things now, understand that it may be because you are a Judah, Jerusalem or Israel. God is working out a salvation for you.

If God allows challenges in your life, understand that He allowed it so that His name will be glorified. When you think you've lost it all, God is still at work; when you think everything stands against you, understand that God is still at work. God does not work the way men work, but He is always at work. And because God is at work you will share your testimony.

There are the horns of the wicked world scattering the destiny of men. The good news however is that there are carpenters of God fraying, restoring, and repairing all broken destinies, broken marriages, broken careers, and broken families.

Friends, whatever have been devastated, whatever you have lost since the year began, whatever that made you to cry silently, whatever made you to keep asking God why, is just for a moment because the divine carpenters are at work and in a short while, you will see the undeniable results. They are lifting the burdens, restoring the destinies of men and giving you testimonies.

But why is God at work?

Because*...the LORD taketh pleasure in his people: he will beautify the meek with salvation. Psalm 149:4*

God is beautifying your life right now. I do not care where you are now, you will end this year very well. I do not care what you are going through, you will surely come over. I do not care what is not working right now, God will work it out. I do not care who is mocking you now, soon they will laugh with you. Rejoice. Celebrate. Laugh because your testimony is just around the corner.

God is still at WORK!

CHAPTER 63

THE BELIEVERS' ADVANTAGES

God has asked me to say to the righteous, it shall be well with him (Isaiah 3:10). Why? Because every believer has an advantage that most other people do not have.

Will a believer face fiery trials? Yes. Will he be judged like other men? Yes. But will he overcome? Yes. Because he has an advantage that makes him succeed where others fail, overcome where others go under and move forward where others are stagnated.

What are these advantages? Jeremiah 1:5–19

1. **Predestination** – There is a preordained plan and purpose for every child of God. None of us came into the world by accident, but by divine design to manifest and fulfil a God ordained plan and purpose. Before we were formed in our mothers' womb, He knew us and gave us a unique assignment called destiny (Jeremiah 1:5). Satan is too late to stop a true child of God to manifest and become all that

God has ordained him to become on earth – except you allow him.

2. **Divine Presence** – God also understands that without him, we can do nothing; predestination may not be realized. So, God decided to be with us, go with us and deliver us from all the wickedness of Satan (Jeremiah 1:8&19). His presence destroys fear, injects faith, devastates Satan and causes every wicked mountain to skip like ram (Psalm 114:1-end). At His presence evil and their agents are driven backwards. God's presence makes all the difference as he goes with us to confirm every word with a sign following (Mark 16:20).

3. **Empowerment** – God knew that Satan will try to stop us from becoming all that He has packaged us to be, so He took a third step to empower us with His word and Spirit for exploits. He ordained us and touched us for impartation of grace (Jeremiah 1:9). He also gave us His word that is able to do everything, create everything, and devastate Satan and all his agents. No wonder He said, as many as received Him, to them gave he power to become sons of God (John 1:12). It takes power to become a true son of God, to make wealth (Deuteronomy 8:18), to trample Satan under our feet (Luke 10:19) and to be a witness (Acts 1:8). These powers He gave to us to ensure we succeed.

4. **Divine Placement** – God does not want any of his plans to fail, so He again, placed us above Satan and his agents. He empowered us and positioned us to pull down all obstacles, destroy all plantings of wickedness, throw down everything

that exalts himself against the knowledge of God and build a new world and plant new vineyards for Christ (Jeremiah 1:10). His placement is far above principalities and powers and over all the power of the enemies (Ephesians 1:21). God has positioned us to make Satan our footstools. You are placed above to always succeed.

5. **His Voice** – God going with us is one thing, us hearing Him guide us is another. For His voice is full of majesty and able to bring about fruitfulness (Psalm 29:3 – end). So, He gave us access to His voice of direction, guidance and leading (Jeremiah 1:11–13). With His voice, we can see our destiny colourful, our future bright and our tomorrow settled. With His voice, we can hear and understand His plans for us at every point of our journey with Him. With His voice we can see better to move faster. He provided us His voice for better performance.

6. **Divine protection** – Since His acts in our lives will trigger envy and jealousy, God also protects and preserves us against the wickedness of Satan. He ensured our total defence by surrounding us with His presence, making us fully defended, unstoppable, un-molestable, unkillable and untouchable (Jeremiah 1:18). That is why He made us all spirits and winds (John 3:8). His angels surrounds us daily, watching over us and ensuring our destinies are kept. He also has a wall of protection around us day and night (Job 1:9). We are therefore too defended to be a victim of Satan and his agents.

Enemies of the Believers Advantage

1. Fear – The greatest enemy of a believer is fear. Fear immobilizes destiny and makes it impossible for a believer to enjoy all the advantages that God has provided for him (Jeremiah 1:6). Fear is a dirty enemy of destiny.
2. Excuses – Another enemy of destiny is excuses which has a way of excusing us from God's blessings (Jeremiah 1:6). It may be a manifestation of fear or may even stand on its own. Avoid it.
3. Laziness – Many have great destinies, but laziness has destroyed them completely. You must therefore gird up your loins, arise and take over or you will be walked over by Satan (Jeremiah 1:17).

Why has God provided these for the believers?

1. Because daily, there are fiery trials in life (1Peter 4:12). Challenges are real, God knows we will face them, so He made provisions for us. The good news is that before the challenge came, God had already made provisions for them. So, they are late in coming.
2. Righteousness is hard. Life throws us with several challenges that make righteousness hard (1Peter 4:18). To scale new heights and even make heaven, we all need God in unusual ways. Thus, the believers' advantages.

CHAPTER 64

GOD'S PRIMARY ASSIGNMENTS TO HUMANITY

God has several assignments to man because man is His prime project and greatest creature. He classified man as 'His workmanship, created in Christ Jesus unto good works." (Ephesians 2:10). To further define who man is, He said that they are a chosen generation, a royal priesthood and peculiar nation (1Peter 2:9). These show how vital and important man is to God and how much God cherishes man. So to conclude, He said that man was created just to show His glory (Isaiah 41:21) – as man is HIS best ever product.

Man is, therefore, very critical to God's program on earth. But what is God's primary assignment to humanity? In my study of Isaiah 49, I came across eleven (11) fundamental assignments of God to man. These include:

1. **It is the responsibility of God to call any man.** I do not mean just calling him/her into ministry, which

is also a calling, but calling him/her into existence. Do you know how many lives that were never called, or that were sacrificed for one that is called? Science tells us that the semen of every man contains tens of millions of sperm cells. Each of these can give rise to a new foetus which will later mature into a child. But usually only one succeeds in fertilizing the ova (egg) for singleton babies. The rest are washed away. Usually, before an ova is fertilized, several other ova are lost in menses and these are also potential children lost. It takes the right ova and right sperm cell to form you. You are, therefore, not a biological accident, but a product of divine planning and predestination. No wonder, He said in Isaiah 49:1 – *Listen unto me…the Lord hath called me from the womb;* No wonder He said concerning Jeremiah that before he was formed in his mother's womb, He knew him (Jeremiah 1:5).

2. **It is the responsibility of God to give you a name…..**V1 - *from the bowels of my mother hath he made mention of my name.* You are called and given a name in the bowels of your mother's womb. Your name is not an accident…God made mention of your name while you were yet in the womb (just as Jesus Christ). Whatever name you answer now was not decided by your parents empirically (although they may think so), but by God. That is why, when God decides to give you a new destiny, He also changes your name.

3. **It is God's responsibility to make us fruitful and productive**…V2 - *…He hasth made my mouth like a sharp sword; ….and made me a polished shaft.*

God makes men what they end up becoming, so He will say to Peter, "Follow me and I will make you...." (Matthew 4:19). However, it is our responsibility to know who we were made to be by discovering our destiny, vision and purpose on earth.

4. **It is God's responsibility to give us our life assignments**...V3 – *And said unto me, Thou art my servant...*Just as every manufacturer decides what his product will do, God also decides for every human being what his/her responsibilities on earth are. If therefore you do not want to lament later in life and labour all your life in vain (V4), you must find out from God what your assignment is on earth. Why did He call you into the world? What roles are you expected to play? What responsibilities are yours to execute? Verse 4 is a true picture of a man who worked so hard, but doing exactly what he was not asked to do.... *:Then I said, I have laboured in vain, I have spent my strength for nought, and in vain:...*

5. **It is the responsibility of God to hear our prayers**...V8 – *Thus saith the Lord, In an acceptable time have I heard thee...*God understands that it is not in man to direct his path, that by strength shall no man prevail, that it is not to him that willeth or to him that runneth, and that the battles of life are not to the strong nor the race to the swift. So God has made provisions for man to depend on Him – through prayers. Thus, it is HIS responsibility to hear when we call. No wonder he is called the God that answers prayers...for unto him shall all flesh come. He therefore requires that we call him in the right time, right way and with a right heart/motive. Only

calls made to right phone number using approved phone lines will be heard...call Him in an acceptable time.

6. **It is God's responsibility to help us**...V8 – *...and in a day of salvation have I helped thee..."* God hears our prayers to help us, to preserve us, establish us and cause us to inherit the desolate places. God is at work 24/7 hearing our prayers so as to make us a praise on the earth. Since He knows that the help of Egypt will fail and in vain shall men help us, He has deliberately made Himself available to us to help us overcome life obstacles, remove shame and improve well-being. God is ready, willing and able to help us. Stop looking at other sources and individuals – God is the only true help. When He helps, destinies are realized from prison houses (v9), hunger and thirst is replaced with divine provisions and prosperity (v10). He opens new doors of blessings and causes frustrations to cease (v11).

7. **It is God's responsibility to comfort his people and show mercy on the afflicted**...V13 - *...for the Lord hath comforted his people...* Right from the ages, God alone provides true comfort. And Jesus came as a comforter and when He was about to depart, He promised another comforter to us (John 14:16, 26; 15:26 and 16:7). God comforts us in all our tribulations, trials and temptations. He comforts us when we are depressed, dejected and despised. He comforts us when there is a physical manifestation of the works of wickedness. He is our comforter.

8. **It is God's responsibility to have mercy on us**... V13 - *and will have mercy upon the afflicted.* By

nature, man is programmed to derail as he has free choices to make. God, being the creator of man, understands this shortcoming and thus provided opportunities for return and restitutions – forgiveness. Only God can forgive and thus show mercy. No wonder He was called 'Son of David'. God shows mercy to sinners and unto those afflicted by Satan, even out of their own mistakes.

9. **It is God's responsibility never to forget us**... V15 – *Can a woman forget her sucking child...yea, they may forget, yet will I not forget thee.* Our walls are constantly before God who will at all times be mindful of us and has covenanted never to forget us.

10. **It is the responsibility of God to provide us with men whose heart He has touched**...V18 – *all these gather themselves together, and come to thee...*No one is created by God to be self-sufficient. God believes in helpers of destinies. So, when he called Moses, He gave him Aaron; when God sent Jesus, He also gave Him twelve, twenty and one hundred and twenty others to work with Him; and when He redeemed Paul, He gave him Barnabas and later Timothy. God has men created and ordained to help us in our life journeys. It is also God's responsibility to bring these men to us, cause us to meet and cause them to work with us, work by us and work for us. As they come, we clothe them as garments and bind them unto us as a bride doeth.

11. **It is God's responsibility to contend with them that contend with us**...V25 – *for I will contend with him that contendeth with thee, and I will save thy children...*Life is full of battles and as we are limited

in our capacity, we have the unlimited God fighting daily for us, contending for us and saving not only our children, but everything that pertains to us. In these battles, our enemies are not only defeated, they are also made to eat their flesh as food and drink their blood as wine – that is, their destruction is permanent and irreversible (v26).

However, as believers, what are our roles towards the realization of these divine responsibilities. God expects us to

1. Mix His word with faith – for without faith, it is impossible to please Him (Hebrews 4:2).
2. To believe in Him and His willingness to execute the eleven fold responsibilities (Hebrews 4:3), so that we can enter into the rest He has reserved for us all (v9).
3. We must labour to enter into the rest God has ordained for us, lest we miss the divine opportunity and fail due to unbelief (Hebrews 4:11). This is labouring in the word of God which is quick and powerful and sharper than any two-edged sword. Understanding of the word procures our rest in every battle of life.
4. Pray our way into His blessings as we enter boldly into His throne of grace to obtain mercy and find grace that will help us even in time of need.

Therefore, everyone of us has a fourfold responsibility to enjoy God's eleven-fold responsibilities – have faith, believe in his provision of rest, labour in the word, and pray your way into His presence and favour.

CHAPTER 65

GUIDANCE ON KINGDOM PROSPERITY

God is rich. He is the owner of the whole earth and the fullness thereof (Psalm 24:1). To ensure we understand this, He also told us that the silver and the gold in the earth are His (Haggai 2:8). He is never in need and thus, does not need anything from any of us.

Becoming His child also qualifies us to becoming rich. So, He takes pleasure in the prosperity of the righteous (Psalm 35:27). And His superior wish is that we prosper and be in health even as our souls prosper (3John 2).

But kingdom prosperity is neither a wish nor a promise. It is a covenant and only those willing to abide by the covenant can access and enjoy this prosperity.

Why Prosperity?

Majority of every Christian's prayer requests can be solved by money – house rent, school fees, hospital bills, house upkeep, clothing, transportation, etc. All are money dependent. Majority are living in shame and reproach because they lack the required resources to make ends meet.

The Scripture admonishes every believer to provide for his family, especially for members of his own household (1Timothy 5:8). It also enjoins us to train up our children in the way that they should go and when they are old they would not depart from them (Proverbs 22:6). But providing for the household and training children are all capital intensive. There are several believers who would have loved to do more if they had the needed resources. But because they have not, they are limited.

To ensure that resources are available for everyone to provide for his household, train up his children and live as kings and priests on earth, God made adequate provisions available for all and has given these to His children (2Peter 1:3-4). However, it is required of us to access these provisions and maximize them for the advancement of the kingdom.

This reflection is therefore programmed to help each of us access these kingdom provisions and by so doing live the kind of life God has ordained for us.

The truth of the Scriptures

Kingdom prosperity is a personal responsibility. It is not an inheritance, it is not a gift of man nor of the Spirit. It is a product of personal responsibility. Leaving in the hands of God what He has given us the power to do for ourselves here on earth is as sinful as rejecting His will when it is made manifest to us. We must take absolute responsibility for our lives if we desire to have the best of life and of God, as "Any faith that makes God absolutely responsible for your life and destiny is an irresponsible faith". (Bishop David Oyedepo).

What is God therefore saying?

Isaiah 48:15: *¹⁵ I, even I, have spoken; yea, I have called him: I have brought him, **and he shall make his way prosperous**.*

God spoke, God called, God brought us all into this world and out of sin and iniquity; but it is our responsibility to make our ways prosperous. Our prosperity therefore is God designed but man decided. Our prosperity is a product of our choices and decisions. It is a product of our works and acts. It is our responsibility.

What is God therefore saying in our access to this God-given kingdom prosperity?

Isaiah 48:16–17 *¹⁶ Come ye near unto me, hear ye this; I have not spoken in secret from the beginning; from the time that it was, there am I: and now the Lord GOD, and his Spirit, hath sent me.¹⁷ Thus saith the LORD, thy Redeemer, the Holy One of Israel; I am the LORD thy God which teacheth thee to profit, which leadeth thee by the way that thou shouldest go.*

1. **Fellowship with God** (vs 16 - *Come ye near unto me...*). Fellowshipping with God qualifies us to be like God (prosperous) and to access what

He has (wealth and riches). It is who we follow that determines what follows us – following God delivers God's kind of wealth and riches to us. As our life is relationship dependent, having God as our associate, makes us associate with riches, glory and honour. Job said, *"Acquaint now thyself with him, and be at peace: thereby good shall come unto thee.²² Receive, I pray thee, the law from his mouth, and lay up his words in thine heart.²³ If thou return to the Almighty, thou shalt be built up, thou shalt put away iniquity far from thy tabernacles.²⁴ Then shalt thou lay up gold as dust, and the gold of Ophir as the stones of the brooks.²⁵ Yea, the Almighty shall be thy defence, and thou shalt have plenty of silver."* (Job 22:21-25). Following God delivers great riches and blessings.

2. **Hear God's instructions** (vs 16 - *...hear ye this;*). The instructions of God make ways in the lives of men. It is God's instructions that deliver a destiny from destructions and devastations of Satan including poverty and lack. His instructions make highways for everyone willing to hear and obey. No instructions, no distinctions. Why? Until we hear God, our world will not hear us. He is saying therefore that there are things to hear which will make us overcome and establish our prosperity. Job again said, *"¹¹ If they obey and serve him, they shall spend their days in prosperity, and their years in pleasures.¹² But if they obey not, they shall perish by the sword, and they shall die without knowledge.* (Job 36:11-12). It takes full, prompt and willing obedience to God to spend our days in prosperity.

3. **Accept the teaching ministries of God:** (vs 17 - *I am the LORD thy God which teacheth thee to profit,*). Until God Himself teaches us, our profiting is only a wish. His teaching guidelines are as contained and outlined in the scriptures – give and it shall be given unto you; as long as the earth remaineth, seed time and harvest shall not cease; (Luke 6:38, Genesis 8:22), etc. His teaching ministry opens one up to the mystery of tithing, offering, giving to the poor, giving to the prophets, giving to parents, giving for the advancement of the church of Jesus and giving for community development. His teaching ministry opens one up to acceptable giving attitude – how to give willingly, cheerfully, heartily and lovingly. His teaching ministry reveals the mystery of watering our seeds with our confessions, words and mental attitude of thanksgiving. Until one is taught by God, profiting is not in view. We must accept the teaching ministry of God to enjoy His provided prosperity.

4. **Accept His leading (vs 17** -*which leadeth thee by the way that thou shouldest go).* It takes the leading of God to access the place of His wealth. It was God that kept the wealth and riches (silver and gold), and only Him can take us there. Concerning Cyrus, He said, *"Thus saith the LORD to his anointed, to Cyrus, whose right hand I have holden, ... to open before him the two leaved gates; and the gates shall not be shut;...[2] I will go before thee, and make the crooked places straight: I will break in pieces the gates of brass, and cut in sunder the bars of iron:...[3] And I will give thee the treasures of darkness, and hidden riches of secret places, that thou mayest know that*

I, the LORD, *which call thee by thy name, am the God of Israel."* He needs to take us by the hand to lead us to where the blessings are kept. No one can access kingdom prosperity without divine leading. It is frustration to try to find it with the energy of the flesh. Peter worked all night, toiled all night without a catch until divine leading in Luke 5:1–5. Also in John 21:1-6, he again worked all night without any results until the Voice guided him to the right side of life. Only the guided can be granted financial prosperity. Be guided.

What are the evidences of kingdom prosperity?

Isaiah 48:18-19, 21- *[18] O that thou hadst hearkened to my commandments! then had thy peace been as a river, and thy righteousness as the waves of the sea:[19] Thy seed also had been as the sand, and the offspring of thy bowels like the gravel thereof; his name should not have been cut off nor destroyed from before me.[21] And they thirsted not when he led them through the deserts: he caused the waters to flow out of the rock for them: he clave the rock also, and the waters gushed out.*

1. **Overwhelming peace**. (vs 18 - *[18] O that thou hadst hearkened to my commandments! then had thy peace been as a river,)* Having resources gives unusual peace. Whenever we are able to pay our bills, meet needs, response to financial request of others, and solve family financial needs, we have peace with ourselves, our spouses, our children, and with our friends. Having the means to meet life's

daily needs delivers peace – peace that passeth all understanding.

2. **Enhanced righteousness**: (vs 18 - *and thy righteousness as the waves of the sea).* Money enhances righteousness as it prevents 'little lies', 'little sins' and even deceits and cheating. Friends, the most holy God is also the wealthiest God. Having what it takes to solve life's problems frees your time and energy to focus on other needs of life – including enhanced spirituality.

3. **Fruitfulness**: (vs 19 - [19] *Thy seed also had been as the sand, and the offspring of thy bowels like the gravel thereof;).* Kingdom prosperity grants us access to fruitfulness on all sides. Let me focus here on bodily fruitfulness (i.e. able to have children). When we have access to resources, even when our bodies are not in line with God's plan, we can procure helps and assistance from doctors and specialists. This requires money! In addition, when we have enough resources, we are at peace and when we are at peace, our righteousness is enhanced and God's word comes to pass – none shall be barren in the land, none shall cast their young or miscarry blessings, etc.

4. **Surplus**: (Vs 21 - [21] *And they thirsted not when he led them through the deserts: he caused the waters to flow out of the rock for them: he clave the rock also, and the waters gushed out.)* Every time God leads, and teaches, He leads us to plenty. Financial thirst is a product of missed guidance and leading. Psalm 23:1-6 tells us what we enjoy when the Lord is our Shepherd, when we allow Him to lead us and

when we follow His leading hook, line and sinker –
to the green pastures, to where the grass is green
and out of every trouble. God's leading destroys
thirst and delivers prosperity.

What therefore is the individual attributes that guarantee access to kingdom wealth?

Hebrews 3:2, 4, 19: *² Who was faithful to him that
appointed him, as also Moses was faithful in all his
house.⁴ For every house is built by some man; but
he that built all things is God.¹⁹ So we see that they
could not enter in because of unbelief.*

1. **Faithfulness**: (vs 2 - *was faithful in all his house*).
   We must be faithful in all that we do. Be faithful
   to our assignments, to our family, to our ministry,
   and to the resources God places in our hands.
   It takes faithfulness to enjoy God's fullness. The
   scripture said unless we are faithful in the little, no
   one will commit unto us the bigger riches, except
   we are found faithful in the unrighteous mammon,
   no one will commit unto us the true riches, except
   we are found faithful in that which is another man's,
   God will not give us our own. Faithfulness is key to
   financial freedom. Remember it is always expected
   that a steward (including stewards of His financial
   blessings) be found faithful (1Corinthians 4:2)

2. **Take responsibility** (vs 4 - *⁴ For every house is
   builded by some man).* Until we take responsibility and
   take steps, nothing will happen. Stop sleeping, stop
   murmuring and complaining, stop comparing your

woes with other people's blessings, just rise up and take steps. God is ready and has been waiting for you. Nothing good happens to an idle hand. Take steps.

3. **Partner with God** (vs 4 - *but he that built all things is God.*). Our skills, competences, connections and personal resources can start, but can never be enough for what God has ordained for us. Therefore, we must partner with God. Begin, but allow God to continue and to complete. God is just waiting for us to take the first steps and He will meet us half way, take over and perfect it. It is God that perfects all that concerns us (Psalm 138:8). But we must start before He can perfect. Take steps, but work in partnership with God.

4. **Belief**: (vs 19 - *[19] So we see that they could not enter in because of unbelief.*) Unbelief, any day, any time is a major hindrance to destiny. We cannot please God without faith (Hebrews 11:6). If we do not please Him, He cannot teach us, He cannot lead us, He cannot partner with us and He cannot therefore help us. Many have not entered their financial rest because of unbelief (Hebrews 4:1-2). We must believe that what He has promised, He is able to do; what He has said, He will perform; if He called us, He also will perform it; and where he leads, He provides. We must believe because unless we believe, we can never become all that He has packaged for us.

Remember that God cares: *"For the Lord taketh pleasure in his people: he will beautify the meek with salvation."* Psalm 149:4

CHAPTER 66

BE A BLESSING

To be blessed, is a right; but to be a blessing, is a RESPONSIBILITY. God gives health as a right but what you use your health to do is your responsibility. For instance, your parents have to pay your tuition fee – this is a right; but what you do in school is your responsibility. In life, there are two kinds of people those that are blessings to others, and those that are burdens. Be a blessing, not a burden,

To be a blessing (or a burden) is a choice. God has blessed many of us tremendously by, but we have refused to be a blessing to others. Blessing is not a function of how much you have, but it is about how willing you are to be a blessing. For instance, if you have $10 and you can't share that with someone, it will be more difficult to share when you have millions.

There are four fundamental reasons why you should be a BLESSING.

1. **Prolongs Relationships**. People commonly desire to separate from you when you are a burden. But if you are a blessing, they will want to stay attached to you forever. Being a blessing prolongs relationship at individual, family, business, and societal levels. It is not a prayer point, but a blessing point. Think of Jacob, Laban with all his wickedness did not want him to go because he was a blessing. Think of Joseph. Potiphar asked him to remain because he (Potiphar) discovered that God had blessed him because of Joseph. What of Ruth and Naomi. Ruth said, (despite losing her husband), "your people shall be my people and your God, my God." Also, Ruth and Boaz, David and Jonathan, etc. If you take a look at the contemporary world today, this also prolongs relationships. In marriage, it is your being a blessing that guarantees your happiness; in career, it is your being a blessing that guarantees your promotion and longevity. Be a blessing.

2. **Preserves Life and Prevents Destruction.** Isaiah 65:8 recorded, *"Thus saith the LORD, As the new wine is found in the cluster, **and one saith, destroy it not, for a blessing is in it;** so will I do for my servants' sakes, that I may not destroy them all."* When there is a blessing in you, you are preserved from destruction. Blessing preserves destinies, careers, marriages, and everything around you from destruction. Why do you keep some clothes and discard others – their usefulness; why do you eat some food and refuse others – their healthiness; why do you wear some necklaces and give out others – most time, their values. We easily destroy

or throw away empty cans and containers, but store cans and containers containing precious things like drinks, food, etc. We retain what is useful and discard or destroy what is useless. If you are useful to an organization, society, family or person, they will not easily dismiss you; if you are useful to your spouse, he/she will not easily divorce you; if you are useful in your neighbourhood, they will always value you. But when you are useless or just a burden, then destruction or displacement is inevitable. Be a blessing not a burden.

3. **Divine Visitation.** In Genesis, God visited Abraham and Sarah was told that she would bear a son because Abraham and Sarah chose to be a blessing to the Angels (unawares). In Acts, Chapter10, Cornelius was described as a man willing to be a blessing to the people. God sent Peter to him to save his entire family. By being hospitable, good, and homely, people have entertained angels unawares that changed their lives forever. When you are a blessing, and not a burden, divine visitation comes.

4. **Delivers you from Death**. Being a blessing delivers you from death. Take for instance, Dorcas in the bible. She died but came back to life on the platform of being a blessing to her world. Her good deed to people spoke for her, and were remembered by the widows, that even after she died, they refused to bury her and went in search of a solution.

If you are a blessing and not a burden, good things will come your way. Many of us are struggling so much because we are burdens, and not blessings to people. Our prayer list is so long just because we are burdens to ourselves and the people around us. In this season, make a decision to be a blessing, let people celebrate God because of your life, let someone, thank God for the day he/she met you, people should be bold to thank God for your presence in their department, life, family, and business.

God's word said, it is more blessed to give than to receive. The main purpose for our lives is to impact our world, and to be a blessing to people around us. Friends, my prayer for us, is that God will give us the Grace to become and remain blessings to people.

CHAPTER 67

RESPECT THE LAW OF DEPENDENCY

Let me introduce you now to the Law of Dependency. This law states that every human being in a state of dependency ALWAYS has a PRICE to pay. The price may vary based on the nature of the dependency and people involved, but there is ALWAYS a PRICE to pay.

The Bible tells us that the words we read and hear are for our examples, instruction, and correction. Therefore, we are to learn from the examples we have read from the Bible. We should implement what worked, and avoid what did not work. This will help us ride on the shoulders of those who have gone ahead of us and avoid the mistakes they made.

The truth remains that if we make the same mistake(s) our forefathers and elders made, it means we are either deaf and dumb, or not learning at all. The book of Esther Chapter One summarized the story of Vashti – the Queen. Vashti began as a queen and ended as a nonentity. The King remembered her in Chapter Two, he was pleased with the suggestion of his officials to replace her and he replaced her with Esther. This will not be our portion.

In life, there is a price for dependency. If you depend on God for anything, there is a price to pay – including that of thanksgiving, worship, praise, service, and stewardship. Similarly, if you depend on someone or anyone for anything, you must pay a price. Vashti was not a queen because she was pretty, but because she was linked to the king. Her throne was dependent on the king and when she despised the king, she lost the throne. Be careful not to despise the source of your blessings.

If we take any God-given privilege for granted, we will be grounded. The king summoned Vashti, but she refused to attend and instead gave excuses. Her excuses maybe genuine, but that did not go down well with the king. At the point the king and his cabinet were discussing how to remove her, she was not there to defend or explain herself. Be very careful. Without you knowing it, people and bodies maybe discussing you right now. This is real and true. Give people and organizations something good to talk about every time.

Understand that excuses are useless in the affairs of life. What people reckon is what you did and or failed to do. They may know that you are incapacitated or deliberately make the work difficult. This may be to give you reasons not to do the work. Be reminded that the moment you fall for this conspiracy, you will become a victim. No matter how good you are, do not ever think that you are indispensable or irreplaceable. Kindly take note of this as you build your families, businesses, career and ministry. No matter how good you are, there is always a David waiting to take over from you. There is always an Esther hungry for your throne. There is always a more qualified replacement out there. Always have this in mind!

We are in a dependency mode with God, that is why we ought to praise and worship Him at all times. We owe Him everything – our lives, skills, resources, families, etc. – in short everything. The bible says, *"Except the Lord build the house, they labour in vain that build it: except the Lord keep the city, the watchman waketh but in vain. It is vain for you to rise up early, to sit up late, to eat the bread of sorrows: for so he giveth his beloved sleep."* *(Psalm 127:1-2).* Similarly, in our various careers, without the help of the helpers of our destinies, we cannot go far.

Friends, we are all in a dependency mode. For instance, in our daily work package, we must work hard to keep our work going even if it requires us to go the extra mile. It is self-defeating to think you are the best or have made it all. There are always people out there preparing for and ready to take over your position. They are planning and preparing, and going the extra miles to take over from you. Do not be caught unawares.

There is always a price to pay when you are in a dependency mode. These prices include

1. **The Price of Obedience:** Obey instruction whether it is comfortable or not; why? Because it is in obedience that you are qualified for God to judge every disobedience against you. Vashti lost because

she refused to obey simple instruction – come and show yourself to the people. Your reasons are never adequate. Just obey. Do you know that most things we lose in life are not because Satan is strong, but because we were disobedient? Be obedient.

2. **The Price of Meekness:** Kill your pride. I am sure you must have heard that we are receivers and never achievers. Everything we are and we have – beauty, height, wealth, health, qualifications, etc. are all gifts from God. Remember, Paul planted, Apollos watered, but God gave the increase (1Corinthians3:6). Also, every house is built by some man, but he that built all things is GOD (Hebrews 3:4). Why are you proud? Kill the pride and take up the yoke of meekness. It takes meekness to obey every instruction and to go the extra mile. Be meek.

3. **The Price of Organization and Reorganization:** Be organized and if needed, reorganize your program to accommodate the demands of your benefactors. Everybody can always have things to do, so being busy is not an excuse. You must know whether what you are busy with will give you what you desire. We should reorganize our time to do the important things first – not necessarily the urgent things. A friend told me that people are missing out in life because they are busy with the 'good' at the expense of the 'best'. Get divorced from the good – good meal, good job, good neighbourhood, good car, good wardrobe, etc. Please go for the best.

4. **The Price of Excellence and Expertise:** Look out for the best way of doing anything. Be innovative. Be creative. Continuously reinvent yourself and

your systems. You must make the decision to stand out from the crowd; you must show that you have something real, unique and tangible to offer that nobody else can offer that same way. You must choose to leave a record of accomplishments.

CHAPTER 68

A SEASON OF HARVEST

The Bible in Joel 3:13 says, *put in the sickle, for the harvest is ripe: come, get you down; for the press is full, the fats overflow; for their wickedness is great.*

Do you know that some people farm without harvesting their produce? I am sure this may come to you as a surprise – but it is true. There are people who work so hard and end up not enjoying the harvest because they never paid the additional simpler price to bring in their harvests - they never put in their sickles.

It is very important to put in the sickle of harvest in any harvest season to harvest your rewards. If you don't put in the sickle, you might end up labouring for nothing. Harvesting requires a decision. It is not a chance occurrence. Also, just as farming is a conscious effort, harvesting requires a conscious effort. You don't harvest by chance, but by choice.

Therefore, put in the sickle! There are three basic sickles required for harvest. These are,

1. **The Sickle of Thanksgiving and Gratitude:** Begin by thanking God for the energy and grace to be alive to harvest. At harvest time, you must be careful about your every word. Many may labour seriously for several days, weeks, months and even years, and destroy everything within an hour by careless talks. Harvest time is the time you should be careful not to use your mouth to kill your seed, but to fertilize your seed and call forth your harvest. If you say what they say, you will see what they see; but if you say what you want, you will get what you want.

   You must use your mouth as a sickle of harvest, calling forth those things that be not as though they were. Until you speak it, the angel will not pick it, and God will not perform it. You must thank God that your prayers are answered and that your season of harvest is here. God is coming quickly with His rewards according to Revelation 22:12*And, behold, I come quickly, and my reward is with me, to give every man according to his work shall be.*

2. **Believe:** It is impossible to receive anything from God without faith. You must believe to become (John 1:12). Hebrews 11:6 further informs us that... ***without faith it is impossible to please him; for him, that cometh to God must believe that he is and that he is a rewarder of them that diligently seek him.***

   You must believe that you serve a God who can and who will do it. A lot of times, we doubt God, and when that happens, you start losing everything you have hitherto laboured to gather. When you start asking questions such as, 'Can this happen?' or 'How will it happen?' When you begin to mourn that God is taking too long to come, you miss Him. God's timing is always the best. It is best to believe in His appointed time. One thing that has kept me going is the fact that I have come to realize that I am too small to make God to fail. Moreover, there is nothing that I need now that God can't provide. If there is a delay in what I asked of Him, it could be my fault. Believe God that He is able, willing and ready to do it for you.

3. **Be Full of Expectation**: When God wants to bless a man or a woman, He does it in three ways: (a) He might send someone your way; (b) he might send something your way like a word or gift; or (c) He might open your mind to an idea, a plan, or a project.

   His words said that surely there is an end and the expectation of the righteous shall not be cut short. Your expectation is God's raw material for your miracles. When you have no expectation, there is no raw material for God to work on.

   Everything you see physically began from things unseen. God will surprise us. So go for your harvest. Put in the sickle.

CHAPTER 69

A LIFE WORTH LIVING

Let us learn from the parable of the girdle as documented in the Bible by Jeremiah.

> *Jeremiah 13:1-7: Thus saith the LORD unto me, go and get thee a linen girdle...take the girdle...and hide it there in a hole of the rock...And it came to pass after many days, ... I went ... and dug, and took the girdle from the place where I had hidden it; and, behold, the girdle was marred, it was profitable for nothing.*

This girdle is like a talent from heaven, and when applied and used, it is beautiful and everyone admires it; but when you hide it, it becomes useless.

Everyone has his or her own God-given girdle. People have different talents, and these are unique. The girdle is also like our lives. If you do not maximize your life, talent, and opportunity, it becomes profitable for nothing.

Every aspect of our life is like the GIRDLE. Many have angelic voices, while some have the skills to write, sell, manage, lead, repair things, clean, or even cook. We are blessed with skills and are free to apply our skills, talents. Do not be limited by the department or unit you are in. If you have skills that can be useful in any department or unit, maximize it. Do not hide your skills, talents or gift. Remember, whatever you do not employ, you forfeit; whatever you do not use, you lose. If you quit, you lose automatically. This applies to everything – whatever you do not use declines, diminishes, decreases, etc. Use and get better.

A life worth living is a life where your talents are not hidden in a hole, but your life is a pathway of making others happy and fulfilled. Most importantly, a life worth living is a life celebrated by people, and emulated by many people. Always have the mindset of leaving a legacy that people won't forget in a hurry in everything you do. How can one live a life worth living? These four things will help you:

1. ***Look for opportunity***: Opportunity comes to you in work apparel. However, if it doesn't come to you, go in search of it. Anywhere you find it, try your best to explore it to the fullest. Sometimes the opportunity that comes to you might be a lesser one. Be proactive. The opportunities you actively search for will always make a difference in your life. Stop doing the same thing repeatedly the same way, expecting a different result. Learn to always look for a better way to do it, look for ways to make your work easier. Develop and use template, guidance, and platforms.

2. ***Expand and stretch***: Learn to do more than your work requires. Learn to go the extra mile. Learn to maximize your spare time and after work hours. Learn to expand and stretch. Many are doing nothing else except what they are told to do. This is wrong, and you will never be the best you are created to be. If your work requires that you resume by 8.00 am and close by 5:00 pm, what do you do with your extra hours – 5:00 pm to 8:00 am? If you do nothing to improve yourself, your income or your work, then you are neither truly expanding nor stretching yourself. To succeed in life, you must stretch yourself in the right direction. The right direction is important because people fail, either because they do not stretch themselves or because they tend to stretch in the wrong direction. There are two kinds of pain, the pain of success and the pain of failure. You must choose which one you want. And stretching is not enough – you must stretch in the right direction, for the right length of time, and with the right amount of energy to achieve your goals. Stretch!

3. ***Fine-tune your gifts into skills***: Gifts are good, but they may not be profitable until they are turned into skills. Raw materials are inexpensive, but refined products are expensive. Nigeria has the habit of exporting raw materials – crude oil, cocoa, palm oil, hinds, and skins, etc. and importing finished products – computers, shoes, etc. Are you still wondering why Nigerians are so poor? Raw materials are CHEAP! Refine your gifts into skills. In fine-tuning your skills, you may sweat – but that will be for a season. After refining it, you will sweat less.

Remember that in life there are people that struggle without succeeding and those that succeed without struggles. Skills make life interesting and minimize struggles and sweats. Pay the price now and enjoy for the rest of your life. Refine.

4. ***Try, Check and Learn (TCL)***: People get better by trying, practicing and practicing again. Therefore, to live a life worth living, try. If you fail, check where you failed, learn from it and try again. Do not give up if you fail because F.A.I.L means "First Attempt In Learning. If you make a mistake once, it is not a mistake but part of your learning curve. However, if you fail to learn from it and continue to repeat it, that is the real failure. Try, check and learn. This is the T.C.L of life.

Therefore, friends let us choose a life worth living by been relevant and maximize the girdle that we have. God bless you.

CHAPTER 70

THE DANGERS OF
A ROTTEN FRUIT

Whether it is a tomato, mango, an apple or whatever fruit – or even a rotten egg, the impact is the same, – it destroys the rest if not taken out immediately. Many good works are wasted because farmers work to protect or preserve a rotten fruit/meat/egg. If rotten, please understand that is it is no longer useful for anything except to be discarded.

Imagine these scenarios: the impact of a drop of kerosene in a pot of soup, rotten egg in an omelette, rotten tomato in a tomato paste, or rotten meat in a pot of stew and soup. Anytime something rotten is added to good things, it messes up the whole bunch.

The same is the situation in human relationships – rotten people mess up the entire team. Wicked people destroy the good works of others. Team member's lies make everyone look like liars. Cheating by a team member makes every member defend themselves against cheats. Falsified program figures by current or out gone staff can hurt current staff and put their jobs at risk. This is the danger of rotten fruit(s).

We need to protect our results, our career, our finances, our families, our ministries, our future from all forms of rotten fruits. The Bible tells us about the effect of rotten fruits in Israel.

When a rotten fruit – Achan, the son of Carmi – entered Israel, Israel lost a battle to a small town named Ai, thirty-six people were killed, and Israel fled before their enemies (Joshua 7:1-26). Because Achan misbehaved, his sons and daughters were stoned to death and buried; and his entire property burnt to appease God. Innocent people were destroyed because of his greed; and he lost – not only the things he took but also the things he worked all his life to acquire including his children. To every sin by an Achan, there is a consequence and many times, it affects other people who were not involved in the act by the doer.

Remember when David was moved to count Israel and the anger of God was kindled, the Lord sent a pestilence upon Israel that killed seventy thousand men (2Samuel 24:1-16). It took David's raising an altar to bring to an end the destruction of innocent souls. Here again, souls were destroyed, but David and his family were preserved.

When Jonah entered into the boat going to Tarshish instead of Nineveh as commanded by God, all those in the ship lost everything they had as they threw their wares into the ocean to save the ship. They would have lost their lives as well, had they not woken up Jonah who was sleeping and had him dumped into the ocean (Jonah 1:3-15). The waves were contrary, the ship was at risk and everything went bad until Jonah (the culprit) was removed from the ship. Surprisingly, God had already prepared a transport for him in the belly of a fish. In most cases, not the people who cause problems lose the most.

Whenever there is a rotten fruit in the midst of good seeds, destruction is inevitable unless the rotten fruit is removed or destroyed. Protecting the rotten fruit or seed will hurt the destiny and lives of the rest. We must remove all rotten fruits around us, and try to rebuild the system to protect the prosperity and posterity of the rest. The strength of a chain is determined – not by the strongest link, but the weakest link. We need to ensure that our weakest links are strong enough to sustain our work and our future – and if not possible, remove and rework the chain.

How to manage rotten fruits:

As people, we need new knowledge to change our attitudes; and a problem cannot be solved if one's knowledge content remains the same as what s/he had at the time the problem was created. There is need to share keys on how to avoid the dangers of rotten fruits in a system. These include:

1. **Be Observant:** Every person has two main roles – understand your role and responsibilities as a person and understand the roles and responsibilities of your co-workers. Doing your work is good but doing just your work is not good enough.
2. **Investigate:** If you see what is not right, investigate – is it real or just a mirage? Explore the various ramifications of what you saw and document

your findings. Work to learn from your observation, and to prevent any negative consequences that may arise from it.

3. **Take Action:** Joshua took action by stoning Achan and his family and burning his property; David took action by raising an altar for God, and the Mariners took action by dumping Jonah into the ocean. We must take action against any individual that want to tarnish our names, efforts and destiny. Do not just pray and wish, take action.

CHAPTER 71

RECOVERING ALL THAT YOU HAVE LOST

In life, what happens to us does not determine our future, but our attitudes and reactions to the issues. Everyone loses things at some point in their lives. It is not what we have lost that is the issue, but how we handle the situation.

Having complained, cried, mourned and asked the question why, it is time to stop, rise and take steps towards recovering all you may have lost. For some, it could be money, health, marriage, career, relationships, business opportunities, children, or even their spirituality. While to some, it could be their resident permit, green card, visa, interview, etc. Whatever it is, enough of mourning and crying – it is time to go out and recover all.

God made the entire earth in six days (Genesis 1:3-30). This came after the devastation of the former world, formless and void with darkness upon the face of the deep (Genesis 1:1-2). God took steps and everything changed in just six days and became very good (Genesis 1:31).

Six days, six weeks, six months and six years are all too much for God to do amazing things in anyone's life, family, organization, or community/nation. For anybody negatively affected by issues and situations of life, crying and mourning are natural. Enough of crying and mourning, it is time to go and recover all.

In Genesis 14:12, *"And they took Lot, Abram's brother's son, who dwelt in Sodom, and his goods, and departed."* Abram did not just cry and mourn, for when he "*heard that his brother was taken captive, he armed his trained servants, born in his own house, three hundred and eighteen, and pursued them unto Dan."* Not only that, *"he divided himself against them, he and his servants, by night, and smote them, and pursued them unto Hobah, which is on the left hand of Damascus."* And then what happened, *"...he brought back all the goods, and also brought again his brother Lot, and his goods, and the women also, and the people."* (Genesis 14:14-16).

The Bible documented a similar experience in 1Samuel 30 when the Amalekites came and burnt David's camp and took away all that he had including his two wives. Again, like a mortal, David cried, and people wanted to stone him; but he encouraged himself in the Lord and went ahead, *"enquired at the LORD, saying, shall I pursue after this troop? Shall I overtake them? And he answered him, pursue: for thou shalt surely overtake them, and without fail recover all."* (1Samuel 30:8). You may have cried, prayed, and have done everything you know how to, and God is saying to you right now, as he said to David, pursue, overtake them, and without fail recover all.

In life, irrespective of what you lost, total recovery is very possible. You can recover all your peace, integrity, God's glory, and rest. Amen! Whatever you have lost in the past days and months will be fully recovered. So, let us go out to recover all. What therefore are the basic steps towards recovering all looking at Abraham and David?

1. **Accept**: Accept that you have lost something good, precious and worthwhile: It is foolishness to pretend as if all is well without first accepting the fact that something important and precious was lost. Accept your losses.

2. **Take stock**: Take stock. You need to effectively and accurately document what was lost - quantitatively and qualitatively. You must understand and document the magnitude of what is lost to be able to put in the required amount of effort to recover all. Remember that they took Lot and his goods, and departed. They also *"invaded the south, and Ziklag, and smitten Ziklag, and burned it with fire; and had taken the women captives, that were therein: they slew not any, either great or small, but carried them away, and went on their way."*(Genesis 14:8, 1Samuel 30:1-2). Take stock of what was lost. Be honest about it.

3. **Develop a plan to recover all**: It takes proper planning to prevent poor performances. Abram armed his trained soldiers; they divided themselves into groups and overtook the enemies. Planning is critical to the successful recovery of all that is lost. David pursued, found a young man and sought his helps and guidance to the enemy's camp. Plan to recover all.

4. **Pursue and Recover:** Just like David and Abraham, take steps to recover all. What you MUST do is go out there, pursue, make a positive move, and then God will magnify your steps and deliver victory to you. *Psalm 18:36-37 says"³⁶Thou hast enlarged my steps under me, that my feet did not slip. ³⁷I have pursued mine enemies, and overtaken them: neither did I turn again till they were consumed.*

5. **Watch out for helpers of destiny**: David and his team found one who led them to their enemies. God positions helpers of destinies along the line – but for only those on the way to recovery. God will put the right people in position, offices, homes, and places that will help you recover everything lost. My prayer is that your eyes shall be open to avoid distraction or traitors.

Rise up, take steps, go and do what you know how to do best, and recover all. However, understand that going with God makes the journey interesting and rewarding. This is why you cannot afford to go alone; you have to go with God who makes all impossibilities become possible. He (God) knows where the things we lost are, and he has the capacity to restore all. Walk with God.

God is sending His angels to work on your behalf. God has seen your heart and knows that your errors are not deliberate, so whatever is working against you shall cease by the blood of Jesus. Even if people are against you, God has a way of making your enemy work in your favour.

It is your season of recovering all. You shall recover your peace, joy, health, fruitfulness, resources, and whatever that has been denied you either openly or in secret.

In this season of recovery, you shall recover all.

EPILOGUE

LET'S KEEP IN TOUCH

Thank you for taking out time to read this book. Is the time well spent? You will gain more by applying the various discoveries to issues of life. Daily use of these revelations will make living more interesting, impactful and refreshing. Do not stop until you arrive at your vision – new heights. Try to read the book over again as insight improves with repeated exposures.

Let's keep in touch. I want to know how the book affects and impacts your life – career, marriage, academics, business, spirituality, and finances. Let's keep in touch.

I want to know the things you changed, habits you altered and risks you took; and what the results were after a few days, weeks, months and years. So, let's keep in touch.

I want to know the way the book affects your ministry, mentorship programs, and trainings. What the outcome and benefits of using the revelations in others are. Let's keep in touch.

You can reach me on +234 809 608 3335, **droleribe@ yahoo.com**, **pastorexcellence@gmail.com** or via my blog **www.obinnaoleribe.com**

Let's go out there and excel as we remain in touch.

God bless you.

Dr Obinna O Oleribe was born into the Anglican Communion, but his search for the truth brought him into Living Faith Church Worldwide where he was ordained a Pastor in July 2008. He is a public health consultant with five fellowships including FRCP and FWACP, a doctorate degree in public health, three master's degrees in public health and business administration, and two bachelor's degrees in pharmacology, and medicine and surgery. He is a multiple award (academic and non-academic) winner. He currently works as a Chief Executive Officer of Excellence and Friends Management Care Center (EFMC) Abuja as well as oversees several other business interests including Modern Health Hospital, Centre for Family Health Initiative, and Excellence and Friends Management Consult. He serves as the West African Consultant to BroadReach Consulting LLC. He is married with wonderful children.

Printed in the United States
By Bookmasters